# ONE

# LIFE

## UNDER

# GOD

THE LIFE UNDER GOD SERIES

# ONE
# LIFE
# UNDER
# GOD

## His Rule Over You

## TONY EVANS

**MOODY PUBLISHERS**
CHICAGO

Interior design: Erik M. Peterson
Cover design: Smartt Guys design
Cover image: Digital Vision

Library of Congress Cataloging-in-Publication Data

Evans, Tony, 1949-
 One life under God : His rule over you / Tony Evans.
   pages cm
 ISBN 978-0-8024-1186-0
 1. Christian life. I. Title.
 BV4501.3.E93133 2014
 248.4—dc23

                                   2014011574

We hope you enjoy this book from Moody Publishers. Our goal is to provide high-quality, thought-provoking books and products that connect truth to your real needs and challenges. For more information on other books and products written and produced from a biblical perspective, go to www.moodypublishers.com or write to:

Moody Publishers
820 N. LaSalle Boulevard
Chicago, IL 60610


1a 3 5 7 9 10 8 6 4 2

*Printed in the United States of America*

# CONTENTS

---

# CHAPTER ONE

# THE PRIORITY OF THE KINGDOM

---

There once was a man who visited the doctor because, as he told the doctor, his entire body hurt. From the top of his head to the bottom of his feet he was in pain. Every single place he touched brought great pain to him.

The doctor looked him over and then said, "Well, this seems very unusual. I don't see anything wrong." He proceeded to ask the man to touch different places on his body such as his forehead, nose, elbow, and knees. Each time the man touched a different place on his body, he cried out in pain. "It hurts, it hurts," the man complained.

After a few minutes of going through this process, the doctor deciphered the issue.

"Sir," the doctor said with a bit of a sigh, "you have dislocated your finger."

While it felt like everything was wrong with this man, only one thing was wrong. His finger was dislocated, thus causing pain any time he touched a different part of his body. If this man could ever fix this one problem, then all of the pain he thought he was going through elsewhere would be fixed as well.

A number of us are going through life with a lot of different issues that are painful, disappointing, or frustrating. We experience this in our world, lives, direction, purpose, relationships, and all else. It seems like the entire thing is a mess. However, the solution for getting all else functioning properly in your life boils down to one primary principle found in God's Word. If you can get this one thing right, you will get everything else right simply because this one thing affects everything else.

The longest sermon Jesus preached while on earth is recorded in the Bible and is called the Sermon on the Mount. This sermon takes up three full chapters (Matthew 5–7), and it is addressed to believers—originally to His disciples. Christ's Sermon on the Mount is primarily a sermon about the kingdom.

The centerpiece of this sermon revolves around one verse.

In fact, this one verse is the centerpiece of kingdom living altogether. We read, "But seek first His kingdom and His righteousness, and all these things will be added to you" (Matthew 6:33).

Before we take a look at the word I want to focus on from this verse—the word "first"—let's visit the concept of the kingdom. We can't understand how to align ourselves underneath God's comprehensive rule if we don't first understand the kingdom where He reigns.

His is a kingdom without borders and a kingdom without time. To apply the rules, precepts, and writs of this world to this very unearthly kingdom would be similar to bringing a horse and polo stick to a football linebacker, and instructing him to get on with it and play. The rules and tools of this earth do not govern the rules of God's kingdom. As King He sets the way it is to both operate and function. There is one Ruler—God. The rest of us are subject to His rule. He sets the standards, makes the laws, determines the consequences, and establishes the blessings.

In God's kingdom power goes to the weak, who recognize their weakness and humbly look to Him. Forgiveness reigns preeminently, and the amount of money matters less than the heart that offers it, as we see in the case of the widow and her mite. Significance in the kingdom is connected to service. Hope comes through helping others who may need it. Destiny is realized while advancing the purposes of the King.

Jesus spoke plainly of the kingdom when He told Pilate the ways of His kingdom do not reflect the ways of the kingdoms on earth: "My kingdom is not of this world."

He said, "If it were, my servants would fight to prevent my arrest by the Jewish leaders. But now my kingdom is from another place" (John 18:36 NIV).

When His followers asked Him to tell them who was the greatest in the kingdom, Jesus pulled a child close to Him and then replied, "Therefore, whoever takes the lowly position of this child is the greatest in the kingdom of heaven." Continuing on—rather than requiring and demanding the pomp and circumstance typically befit for a King—He instructed His subjects how He would like to be approached as their Ruler and Lord: "And whoever welcomes one such child in my name," Jesus said, "welcomes me" (Matthew 18:4, 5 NIV).

Unfortunately, many of us either don't understand the kingdom or have chosen to live our lives apart from it. We are living as followers of a King whom we seek to dethrone, though maybe not outright, through more subtle ways of complacency, autonomy, independence, or simply through a lack of a connection to Him, His Word, and His rule.

As a result, we experience what anyone in any kingdom living apart from the rules of the King would—in our personal lives, homes, churches, communities, and nation: the chaos that comes from rebellion.

In a kingdom life is to be lived under the rule and authority of the King. The blessings of the covenant of our King in His Word, imbued with the authority He gives us through His promises and His *chesed* love, come when we live all of our life under God. Our King and His kingdom have an agenda, and that agenda is His comprehensive rule over every area of life.

The beginning point for living according to God's kingdom agenda can be found in the word from the passage we opened the chapter with: "first." It is the diminishing of the value of "first" that has led to the diminishing of the experience of God's best in many, if not most, areas of our lives.

## SEEK YE FIRST

To live life to its fullest and to accomplish and experience all God created you to do, God and His kingdom must be first. God is not to be one among many; He is to be first. The problem in most of our lives today is God is merely in the vicinity; He is not first. I often hear people tell me they don't have enough time for God—which means they are really telling me God is not first place in their lives. This is because a person will always make time for what is first, for what matters most.

Over and over in Scripture we read about God and the offering where He asks for the "first fruits" of all He has given us. As just one example of many, we read in Proverbs, "Honor the LORD from your wealth and from the first of all your produce . . ." (Proverbs 3:9). When Jesus reproved the church at Ephesus, as recorded in the book of Revelation, He chided them for having left their first love (Revelation 2:4). Jesus wasn't saying they didn't love Him at all. In fact He applauded them for being upstanding people who have "perseverance and have endured for My name's sake, and have not grown weary" (v. 3). What He was saying is they had left their first love. They no longer regarded Him as first in their hearts or in their lives.

In Colossians, this point of Christ's preeminence over all things is further emphasized where we read, "He is also head of the body, the church; and He is the beginning, the first-born from the dead, so that He Himself will come to have *first place* in everything" (Colossians 1:18). God makes it clear here and repeatedly throughout Scripture that He belongs first in our lives.

Many of us who own homes have what are called "living rooms." However, these rooms are misnamed. They should be called "visiting rooms," because the majority of us live in the den, kitchen, or family room. I remember when I was growing up in Baltimore if I stepped foot in the living room I was quickly told, in no uncertain terms, to get out of it immediately. In fact, even now when I go back to visit, no one lives in that living room at all. It's barely used and still has plastic covering the furniture. This is because the living room to many people is simply reserved for special times or special guests. It is called the living room few people ever live in. It is misnamed.

Many of us have misnamed God. We call Him "Lord God," but He is only good for the visiting room in our lives. We visit Him on Sunday, and we visit Him in our devotional times, but we do not hang out with Him. We do not live with Him. We do not spend the majority of our time in His presence. What is missing for so many people is the principle of *first*. Jesus said we are to "seek *first*" God and His kingdom, above all else in our lives.

Friend, when the God you acknowledge is not treated as God, you cannot experience His kingdom and its benefits. The follow-up portion of the verse we are looking at states clearly that when you put God first, "all these things" will be given to you. The corollary of that rings true as well—when you do not put God first, you are missing out on all of the benefits and blessings of the King and His kingdom. That doesn't mean you won't have problems or issues in life. What it does mean is you will be well equipped to overcome or get through those problems and issues when all of life is aligned under His authority and His rule.

## WHAT IT LOOKS LIKE TO PUT GOD FIRST

One of the major determining factors to know if you are putting God first in your life is to ask yourself where you turn when you have a decision to make. When you have a problem to resolve, or you need guidance, do you turn to people first? Do you turn to your desires first? Or do you look to God, His Word, and His principles first? Getting God's perspective on a matter and then applying it to the particular situation you are dealing with is one revealer of God's position in your life.

If you are a parent, do you recall saying these words to your children: "Why didn't you talk to me first? I just wish you would have talked to me first." Often parents will let their children know they could have avoided mistakes or problems in life if they would have sought and followed their parent's advice first. While this holds true in parenting, it holds even more true with God. So many people wonder why they are not hearing from God or experiencing His abiding presence and victory in their lives. God's answer to their question is simply, "Because you come to me last. In fact, you go to the world—a system that leaves me out—first. And you only come to me when none of that works out."

The key to kingdom success is found in this monosyllabic word *first*. The prioritization of the rule of God over every area of life is where the power of kingdom living is found.

THE PRIORITY OF THE KINGDOM

## PRIORITIZING THE KINGDOM

The context in which we read Matthew 6:33 is critical to understanding it. When we look at the surrounding verses, we can see a recurring theme appearing. We read:

> "For this reason I say to you, do not be **worried** about your life. . . ." (v. 25)
> "And who of you by being **worried** . . ." (v. 27)
> "And why are you **worried** . . ." (v. 28)
> "Do not **worry** then . . ." (v. 31)
> "So do not **worry** . . ." (v. 34)

Did you catch the theme? Yes, worry. Right in the middle of multiple verses addressing our human tendency to worry, God places the very solution to our worry. He says if you will seek His kingdom first and His righteous standards first, He will grant you all of the things that often make themselves the focus of your worry.

Friend, you ought to put God's kingdom first if for no other reason than to reduce your personal anxiety and worry. Over forty million US adults suffer from a diagnosed form of anxiety. Countless millions more no doubt suffer from worry or anxiety on less severe levels. Worry is a common issue plaguing people today. Whether it's worrying about jobs, safety, health, relationships, flying, income, terrorism, the future, or anything else—worry rots away at many people's ability to enjoy the gift of life God has given them.

God tells us in this foundational principle for kingdom living that we actually don't have to worry at all. God Himself—seeking His kingdom and His righteous standards—is the very antidote to worry. In Matthew 6:33 we discover the one principle that affects everything—even the level of your worry.

A man was running late and rushing to catch his plane at the airport. Worried he might miss his flight, he started weaving in and out of the crowd with moves that would make Adrian Peterson proud. Bumping into a man dressed in a flight uniform, the passenger paused briefly to say he was sorry. The uniformed man asked him why he was rushing and he told him that he was trying to catch his flight.

"Where are you going?" the man in the flight uniform asked.

"I'm going to Austin," he replied.

"Well relax and stop worrying," the man said with a smile. "Because I'm the pilot and that plane won't go anywhere without me."

Immediately the man who had been running through the airport, worried about missing his flight, was able to slow down and rest. This is because he knew where the pilot was. Knowing where God is located—knowing what He promises when you look to Him first—will change your anxiety, frustration, irritation, and exacerbation on all levels.

Of all of the problems you face—whatever the category —and of all of the issues that keep you in perpetual defeat . . . have you placed God first in that area? Have you looked to honor Him first in your heart, attitude, choices, and thoughts? Have you sought His wisdom and will for you on how you are to respond to that situation? If you haven't, go ahead and worry, because you will need to worry. But if you have, then rest—God's got it.

## YESTERDAY, TODAY, AND TOMORROW

Chapter six of Matthew closes with the verse that many of us have found easier to commit to heart rather than commit to practice. It says, "So do not worry about tomorrow; for tomorrow will care for itself. Each day has enough trouble of its own" (v. 34).

Most people are being crucified between two thieves: yesterday and tomorrow. They kill today because of what happened yesterday, and they are too scared today because of what may happen tomorrow. Do you know that today is the tomorrow you worried about yesterday? In other words, as long as you are on earth you will never run out of tomorrows. There will always be a tomorrow. So until you learn to make today what today is supposed to be—to embrace today, seize it —you will perpetually live your life either bound by yesterday or tomorrow or even chained between both.

Friend, I would like to challenge you to change one thing and watch that one thing change everything else. When you put God first, all else will fall in place. Make Him first in your thoughts, hopes, and decisions. Put Him first in how you spend your time. Place Him first in how you view the world around you. Please Him first, honor Him first, give to Him first . . . and all else will get in line.

God doesn't say that to put Him first is a request. This is a demand from a deserving King. But when you choose to obey this principle you will reap the benefits of the abundant life Christ came for you to have. In other words, God's got your back when you put Him first.

A lot of people never get to see what it looks like when God has their back because they are out there trying to fix it, solve it, tweak it, and obtain it all by themselves. We are tangling with the Gentiles in a Gentile-run world, and we never truly experience God overruling our issues—simply because we don't put Him first. This is His kingdom and He is the rightful King; putting Him anyplace other than first is foolishness.

Keep in mind we are to seek His "kingdom" and His "righteousness." *Kingdom* means His authoritative rule along with the visible demonstration of it comprehensively in every area of life. *Righteousness* is the standard God requires for people to be rightly related to Him. It includes abiding by the governing guidelines He has set as the King.

In other words, if you are a kingdom Christian and you want to know the right way to go, think, act, perceive, react, or relate—that is called righteousness. Righteousness simply defined is God's standard for living life. His kingdom and His righteousness are to be what each of us seeks first. Without them we are wandering aimlessly around without the support and the backing of our King.

In baseball, if you miss first base when you are rounding the bases it doesn't matter whatever else you do. If you have run past first base without touching it, it doesn't mean anything that you touch second, third, or home plate. It doesn't matter that everyone in the stands is cheering you or congratulating you when you cross home. Because if you miss first base, then nothing after that even counts.

In kingdom living, if you fail to seek God's kingdom and His righteousness first, all else is for naught simply because He has established His rightful place as first and without it you are on your own.

## COMMITMENT AND PRIORITY

When you look around at the Christian community today, you frequently see chaos. Marriages are falling apart, singles are struggling to be content. Debt rules. Addictions run amuck. And yet so many people are faithfully in church leaving many to conclude, "My Christianity is just not working."

They are worn out, lonely, miserable, and frustrated, to say the least.

Many have come to conclude either this thing called Christianity is not real or it is simply not real for them. However, there is a reason why so many well-intentioned believers are falling short of God's best in their lives. This is because without the password called priority, they cannot access all God has in store for them.

If you have a smartphone, it is likely you have a password restriction so if you inadvertently left it somewhere a stranger —or a friend—couldn't pick it up and take advantage of the personal information. Passwords are often critical to the whole process called access, and the password for victorious kingdom living is this word: *First*.

I've talked a lot about the concept of first in this chapter, but perhaps you are wondering, "Tony, what does that look like? How do I do this?" In one of my favorite chapters in Scripture, Paul gives us the visual illustration of what it means to put God first. We read,

> "Therefore, I urge you, brothers and sisters, in view of God's mercy, to offer your bodies as a living sacrifice, holy and pleasing to God—this is your true and proper worship. Do not conform to the pattern of this world, but be transformed by the renewing of your mind. Then you will be able to test and approve what

God's will is—his good, pleasing and perfect will."
(Romans 12:1, 2 NIV)

The problem with many Christians is, while they have made a decision to become a Christian by trusting in Jesus Christ for their salvation, they have not yet made a decision to become a disciple. They have not surrendered their lives to be a committed follower of Jesus Christ. The difference between a decision-maker and a follower is simply ***surrender***.

What Paul is telling us in this passage is God wants us to present ourselves to Him. He wants you to put yourself on the altar. You are to present your life—that means all of you—to Him on His altar. Keep in mind in the Old Testament times, when a sacrifice was placed on an altar, the priest did not just put the head or the arm or a portion of the lamb on the altar. He put the entirety of the being on the altar. What too many believers have done is put a portion of their time, talents, and treasures on God's altar and assumed it is enough. It is not. God wants all of you to be given to Him.

Throughout Scripture we read anytime God wanted to do something big for His people He always required a sacrifice first. There had to be something present that demonstrated sincerity and commitment. Worship is not simply singing songs on a Sunday. True worship, as outlined in Romans 12, is giving yourself to God in your entirety. True worship includes surrender.

I like the story of the chicken and the pig. Both are walking down the street one day when they come to a grocery store with a sign in the window that reads, "Bacon and Eggs Desperately Needed." The chicken looked at the pig and said, "I'll give them the eggs if you'll give them the bacon."

The pig stared back at the chicken and replied, "No way."

The chicken asked, "Why not?"

The pig stated, "Because for you it's a contribution, but for me it's my life."

Unfortunately today we have too many Christians who are only willing to give God an egg here or there, and after they do so they think they've given enough. Or another thing believers will do is climb up on the altar and then climb back off. They wonder why God isn't showing up miraculously in their lives. The reason why He is not is God has asked us as kingdom followers to climb up on His altar and give Him our all.

Our King has asked each of us to live our lives as a "living sacrifice." Quite literally a sacrifice is a dead-thing. So the truest interpretation of this term is we are to be a "living, dead-thing." We are to be alive to God and His desires while simultaneously being dead to our sinful nature and our own will.

## RELATIONSHIP OR RELIGION?

What we need to carefully distinguish, as we look at putting God first and offering our lives in total surrender to His kingdom and His righteousness, is that what we do is rooted in relationship rather than rules. Too frequently people will confuse structure for surrender. They cross off a list and think they have put God first. In all actuality, if God is first you don't need a list because you will naturally seek Him, His heart, and His way in your own personal surrender out of love.

Whenever religious activity, however sincere, trumps relationship, the victory of Christ is no longer experienced in the believer's life. One of the greatest dangers in our churches today is for religion to replace an intimate relationship with the Savior. By religion I am referencing the external adherence to exercises, codes, or practices in the name of God yet apart from God. For example, if you go to church because it is the religious or spiritual thing to do rather than because you are motivated to spend time worshiping God, learning about Him, and experiencing Him, then that is religion. Religion is anything you do for God that does not stem out of a heart connected to God.

One of the assignments I had to do at seminary involved writing a research paper. I remember this particular paper because, when I turned it in, I was very proud of the work I had put into it. I had done my due diligence. I had controlled the material, analyzed all of the possible idiosyncratic elements of the vicissitudes in the arguments. I felt great about my paper.

However, when I got my paper back from my professor there was a big, fat, red zero at the top, along with a smaller note at the bottom. In a hurried hand my professor had scrawled, "Tony, great work. Great preparation. Wrong assignment."

It wasn't that I hadn't done great work; it was I had done my great work on the wrong assignment. I had researched the wrong topic. As a result I didn't get credit for what I had done. Kingdom living is no different. It's not that there aren't a lot of people doing a lot of excellent things. It's not that a lot of these same people attend church, help the hurting, or say all the correct spiritual platitudes. It's that they've missed the priority of the kingdom. They've missed the relational connection that comes through voluntary surrender. They have not made God first in their hearts. And then they wonder why they aren't experiencing any victory, power, hope, and authority in their lives.

External observances—the rules of religion—can get in the way of a relationship. When you are motivated by relationship, surrender comes naturally. There is a story about a woman who was married to an ungrateful, controlling, and dominating man. She had been married to him for over twenty years. It didn't take her long when she first got married to realize unless she did everything on his list, her life would be miserable. She would be yelled at, shoved, and then neglected.

This forlorn woman kept a list in the top drawer of her bureau of everything she knew her husband wanted from her. Every day she would seek to cross off each item on the list. After twenty or so years of marriage, and what seemed like a lifetime of trying to please someone who could not be pleased, her husband died suddenly of a heart attack.

A few years later, this woman met and fell in love with a kingdom man. This man treated her with respect, honor, and dignity. She loved his personality, his heart, and everything about him. She always considered herself to be a lazy woman, because it would take so much effort every day to try and cross off her previous husband's list. She lacked the motivation to do it—and although she did do it, she assumed she must be lazy since she ultimately didn't want to be doing what she was doing.

But life with her new husband shed light on who she was. She had energy, focus, and diligence. In fact, in any given day she would do far more than what was ever on the list for her previous husband, and what's more she would do it both willingly and gladly.

One day, while cleaning out her bureau, the woman found the old list. Noticing that everything on it used to be a chore and had now turned into a pleasure, she wondered what had changed. Then she realized the simple truth that relationship was a far greater motivation than rules could ever be.

The first man dominated through rules without relationship. The second man offered her a relationship that then motivated her response. The activity was the same—in fact, it was identical. But the motivation changed both the results and rewards of the activity.

God wants to be first in your life as your King, but He wants His relationship with you to be the motivating factor for your surrender. Otherwise you are simply begrudgingly crossing off a list called religion and failing to access the strength, peace, and power that comes by way of His love.

We serve a mighty God who is all-powerful, but never forget He is closer than you think. He cares for you. His love is to be your driving passion in putting Him first. God doesn't want you serving Him only because you are supposed to. He wants you serving Him because you love Him. He wants your morality, prayer life, dedication for Him, and all else to be predicated on your relationship with Him rather than on religious duty. Instead of being defined by what you do, He wants you to be defined by who you know—Jesus Christ.

## TWO CRUCIFIXIONS

When you place yourself on the altar as a living sacrifice, you are mirroring Christ's sacrifice on the cross. Essentially there are two crucifixions that must occur in order to experience victorious kingdom living—Jesus' and your own. Paul writes of these, "But may it never be that I would boast, except in the cross of our Lord Jesus Christ, through which *the world has been crucified to me, and I to the world*" (Galatians 6:14, emphasis added).

To identify with Jesus Christ is to identify with His own surrender. Being crucified with Him creates a resultant disconnect from this world's order as well as a subsequent attachment and alignment with Him.

The word "world" in the Greek is *Kosmos*. It simply refers to an organized world system or arrangement designed to promote a specific emphasis or philosophy. For example, we will often talk about the "world of sports," or the "world of finance," or the "world of politics." These phrases are not referencing a location or a place. They are referencing an organized system inclusive of certain definitions, regulations, and philosophical worldviews.

When Paul states he has been crucified with Christ, he is saying he is no longer alive to this world's system that wants to leave God out, or to worldliness. He is crucified to the strategies and rules that are set up to try and make humanity acceptable to God independently of God.

I don't know if you've ever noticed this, but the world does not mind religion. The world not only tolerates religion, but it frequently will even embrace it. Religions dominate much of humanity's systems all across the globe. What the world will not tolerate, however, is the person of Jesus Christ. As soon as you introduce Jesus into the equation, you have become too specific. Staying with God is okay because that is generic and vague. But once you bring Jesus to bear on a life or a kingdom worldview, that is too narrow for many people.

The more religious you become, the further from Christ you go. Putting God first equates a relationship where you willingly surrender yourself as a "living sacrifice" to the One you love. You, like Paul, die daily.

As he pointed out in his letter to the Corinthians, "I affirm, brethren, by the boasting in you which I have in Christ Jesus our Lord, *I die daily*" (1 Corinthians 15:31). Surrender represents the moment-by-moment connection to and identification with Jesus Christ and the purpose of His life, death, burial, and resurrection. It is acknowledgment of complete and total dependency on Christ and His sufficiency in your life.

Jesus wants to be more important to you than your own comforts, wants, and will. Luke says a similar thing to Matthew when he writes in chapter 14 verse 27: "Whoever does not carry his own cross and come after Me cannot be My disciple."

Unfortunately today, we have some messed-up ideas about what it means to carry our crosses or to put God first. A physical problem, bad in-laws, or noisy neighbors—none of those things is a cross. So what does it mean to carry your cross?

When the Romans wanted to put a condemned criminal on public display to humiliate him, they paraded him down the street carrying the crossbeam of his cross. Carrying your cross to the place of execution was a public display that you were guilty of the crime for which you were condemned.

To carry your cross means to bear the reproach of Jesus Christ. It is to be so identified with Him that when they accuse you of being a Christian, you are found guilty. When someone accuses you of being His disciple, you say, "You got me."

To carry your own cross is to admit publicly you are guilty of the crime of being committed to Christ, guilty of placing Him first.

Carrying your cross is when a girl tells her boyfriend, "I can't sleep with you because I am a Christian." It's when a businessman says, "I can't do that unethical thing, because I am Christ's disciple. I am living by a different agenda." Carrying your cross is dying to yourself and what you want and putting Jesus first. It's not comfortable to carry a cross.

Religion and religious titles mean nothing. External paraphernalia and religious duties, when placed against the backdrop of the preeminence of Christ, count for nothing. What matters is your identification with God's kingdom and His righteousness and the newness of the life He now lives within you.

Paul tells us more in his letter to the Galatians, "For neither is circumcision anything, nor uncircumcision, but a new creation" (Galatians 6:15). He writes elsewhere similarly in his letter to the Corinthians, "Therefore if anyone is in Christ, he is a new creature; the old things passed away; behold, new things have come" (2 Corinthians 5:17). Your victory in your daily life, decisions, emotions, finances, and in all things completely hinges on your attachment to Jesus Christ and your relational surrender to Him. It rests on His work, not on your own. It is tied to the new creation within you, not to the flesh.

## THE BENEFIT OF PUTTING GOD FIRST

Paul concluded his letter to the believers in Galatia with this final thought reflecting on the fruit of living a kingdom life of surrender. He writes, "And those who will walk by this rule, peace and mercy be upon them, and upon the Israel of God" (Galatians 6:16).

Why does God often feel so far away? Because we are not operating by this rule. Paul says if you walk according to the rule of surrender—to align your framework of thinking, moving, and operating with the "firstness" of Him and His kingdom, you will experience the benefits of God, which include both peace and mercy. However, when you are merely satisfied with religion or religious activity—or even when you have placed your trust in your religious activity to earn favor with God—you have been severed from Christ and fallen from grace (Galatians 5:1–4).

Fallen from grace is a fairly drastic occurrence. Grace is the provision of all that you need in order to live a life of abundance and peace. To best understand what it means to be "severed from Christ" or to be "fallen from grace," I need to compare it to electricity. Electricity is the flow of power that makes everything work in your home. Virtually everything in your house operates because of electricity. Your appliances, lights, heat, air conditioning, computers, television, and many things work because they are receiving electricity.

If you are severed from electricity, the flow of the power stops even though you still own the appliances, lights, heater, air conditioning unit, computers, television, and all else. It's not that you no longer possess these items nor is it that you didn't pay for and purchase them. But you can have something you have paid for and not enjoy it  because the flow of electricity is no longer there.

To be severed from Christ or to fall from grace means what God wants to do in you and through you is no longer flowing. You have essentially been unplugged, or disconnected, from the power of Jesus even though you still have all of the paraphernalia of religion. Therefore your hope is gone, your peace is gone, your courage is gone, your faith is gone, and your authority is gone.

Yet those who function by the rule of surrender in kingdom living will experience a peace that passes understanding. The Spirit of God will permeate all you do so you begin to think differently, act differently, live differently, love differently, and even recognize yourself in a different light. This is because the flow of the Spirit, the electricity that comes to each of us by way of the accomplishment of the cross, will empower you. God will be at work in you, with you, through you, to you, and for you.

Without electricity, a lot of what you own in your home would be unusable, even though it may have been expensive. Electricity is essential to empowering what was made to run on it. A relationship with Jesus Christ and His sacrifice, my friend, is essential to both empowering and enabling you to live an abundant, victorious life defined by both peace and mercy.

Never let religion get in the way of your relationship with Jesus Christ. Instead, out of your relationship with the One who loves you most, put first things first and watch that solitary decision change everything else for the good of your own life, the betterment of others, and the advancement of God's kingdom agenda on earth.

# CHAPTER TWO

# THE PROCESS OF SPIRITUAL GROWTH

If I asked you to tell me who you are without giving me your name, your occupation, your title at work, or anything else like that, how would you answer?

How you answer that question says a lot about you. It lets me know if you really know who you are. In the Bible when people came to Jesus Christ and were dead serious about following Him, when they became people of the kingdom, there was no question about who they were.

Those early disciples became known even among unbelievers as people of "the Way" (Acts 19:9) because they had chosen to walk a different path in life. They had identified themselves totally with Jesus Christ and the kingdom of God. They lived for the kingdom, and their identity was tied to the kingdom.

The great tragedy today is we don't have enough Christians who know who they are. They may be genuine believers, but their faith is just another addition to their portfolio. When it comes to the bottom line, they define themselves in terms of their name, their job, their possessions, or the people they know.

If somebody asked you who you are and nowhere in the conversation did the name and kingdom of God come up, you are a confused Christian. As a member of the kingdom, your identity is all tied up and wrapped up with Christ. There should be no way to talk about you and not talk about Him.

In other words, for us the term *Christian* is not just a title. It is our identification, just like our name is. Being followers of Christ is the essence of who we are.

That's why we need to understand and cultivate a kingdom mentality on our personal lives. We need to become mature, fully functioning men and women of the King. This is achieved by a process called spiritual growth. Often our spiritual growth takes place through another process called discipleship, which Jesus commissioned us to do while on earth. Each of us must learn how to function within this new kingdom realm that we are in as followers of Jesus Christ, and the learning process is called discipleship. The goal of spiritual growth is to be transformed into the image of Christ so we are consistently increasing in reflecting His character, conduct, attitudes, and actions in our lives. When the Scripture is applied and the power of the Holy Spirit invoked, spiritual development and transformation are inevitable (2 Corinthians 3:17,18).

## JESUS AND DISCIPLESHIP

If you want to find out what mattered most to someone, read his last words. Usually whatever a person considers to be most important is on his mind when he comes to his last days on earth. That's why we pay so much attention to last words, especially of people important to us.

As those who seek to be obedient followers of Jesus Christ, we need to know what matters most to Him so it can matter most to us. Thankfully, we don't have to wonder about it. After His resurrection from the dead and just before His ascension back into heaven, Jesus told His disciples—and us—what was uppermost on His mind. His last words on earth are recorded for us in Matthew 28:18–20.

Notice verse 19: "Go therefore and make *disciples* of all the nations." There it is—stated in clear and concise terms: we are to disciple the people of God (in the church age through the local church) so that they affect the world for Christ. If Christ's mandate for the church is to make disciples, then His will for us as individual believers is that we would become disciples through the process of personal spiritual growth.

To grow spiritually as a disciple of Christ means we become like Him. That's why Jesus said in Matthew 10:25 "It is enough for the disciple that he become as his teacher." Becoming a disciple is where we ought to be heading in our Christian lives.

Let me clarify something before we go much further. Being a disciple, getting down to the essentials of the Christian life, is a lot different than going to church once or twice a week. To get excited because the preacher moved you and the choir inspired you is nice, but that's not spiritual growth.

The goal and the cornerstone of our activity, what brings God the most glory, is for us to become disciples. God's goal is not salvation; that is just the introduction to God's goal. His desire is that those who are saved become disciples.

It is not enough to say, "I'm on my way to heaven." The issue is are you becoming like the One who is taking you to heaven? That's discipleship, and that's what Christ wants from us.

Discipleship is that *developmental process that progressively brings Christians from spiritual infancy to spiritual maturity so they are then able to reproduce the process with someone else.* The singular, overarching goal of a disciple is to bring all of life under the lordship of Jesus Christ and then help someone else do the same.

Notice this brings discipleship around full circle. Disciples are to turn around and make other disciples. Ultimately that's how we fulfill the mandate of Matthew 28:18–20.

## A LEARNER

Discipleship was not a new idea in the New Testament times. It was a well-established concept in the Greek world in the centuries before Christ. The word *disciple* means "learner, student," and the Greeks had disciples in the realm of philosophy.

Plato, often called the "father of philosophy," developed a system of thought that dealt with issues of epistemology, or how we gain knowledge, and issues related to the meaning of life. Plato discipled his student Aristotle, who took what he had learned and built "gymnasiums," or academies.

In the ancient world, gymnasiums were not arenas for sporting events. They were training centers to teach students Plato's thought and the system developed by Aristotle, known as Aristotelian logic. The students thus trained were "gymnatized," which is the verb form of the Greek word for gymnasium.

So successful was this discipling process that it allowed the Greeks to influence the whole Greco-Roman world. This process was called "Hellenization," in which people who were not Greek began to adopt Greek thinking, language, and culture. That was all part of this concept of discipleship.

The New Testament picked up this concept and put it in a spiritual context so we would know what it means to be a disciple of Jesus Christ. Discipleship involves an apprenticeship. The apprentice, or student, is brought toward a particular goal.

In Matthew 10:24–25, Jesus described what a disciple should look like. We read, "A disciple is not above his teacher, nor a slave above his master. It is enough for the disciple that he become like his teacher, and the slave like his master."

Since *disciple* means learner, a disciple is a student who follows the teachings and pattern of another so closely the student becomes a clone of the teacher, to use a modern-day term. We could also call a disciple an apprentice—someone who stands at the side of a skilled master in a trade to learn that trade thoroughly.

The very definition of discipleship shows it can't be accomplished all at once any more than a baby can become an adult overnight. Becoming a disciple is a lifelong process, but that doesn't mean we can kick back and glide for a while.

You may not be where you want to be in your spiritual growth, but you ought to be bigger spiritually this year than you were last year. You ought to be further down the road this year than you were last year. A disciple should always be growing.

## LOOKING LIKE CHRIST

The goal of discipleship is conformity to the Savior, being transformed into the image or likeness of Christ (Romans 8:29).

A pastor friend of mine was visiting a college campus a number of years ago. He didn't know that my son Anthony Jr. was a student there. He said he was walking across campus and saw a young man off in the distance.

My friend said he looked and then stopped dead in his tracks. "That has to be Tony Evans's son," he told himself. "He looks like Tony; he's built like Tony; he even walks like Tony."

He was right, of course. The young man he had spotted was Anthony. Even though the man was a long way away, Anthony's characteristics were so obviously like mine that my friend told me, "I didn't even know Anthony was in college yet. All I knew was nobody could look that much like you and not be yours."

Let me tell you: people ought to be able to see you from a long way off and say, "That person has to be a follower of Jesus Christ." They ought to be able to tell by the way you walk and talk, by the total orientation of your life, that you belong to Christ because nobody could function the way you function and not know Him.

The family resemblance ought to be obvious. It ought to be clear where you stand. That is discipleship. It means to pattern your life after Christ, to follow Him so closely, that you speak, act, and think like Him.

Failing to follow Christ as His disciple means we will meander through a mediocre Christian life rather than living a kingdom life. We will become like the farmer who was teaching his son how to plow.

The farmer told his boy, "Son, I want to plow a straight furrow from one end of this field to the other."

The son asked, "But how will I know when I am plowing it straight?"

"Do you see that cow lying down over in the next field?" the father replied. "Just keep your eye on that cow and plow straight toward her. You'll be fine."

The farmer came back about an hour later and saw furrows going every which way. He couldn't believe it. "Son, what in the world happened? I told you to keep your eye on the cow so you could plow a straight furrow."

"Dad, I did keep my eye on the cow. But the cow kept moving!"

Actually, I don't know any farmer who would advise his son to plow using a moving object. But the point is worth making. If you focus on the wrong object, your life is going to wander all over the place.

You won't have consistent spiritual victory. You'll be up one day and down the next day. But if you're following Jesus, you'll plow a straight line. He's not going anywhere. He is the same yesterday, today, and forever (Hebrews 13:8).

## RIGHT INFORMATION
## COMBINED WITH THE RIGHT SKILLS

Since a disciple is basically a student, one aspect of discipleship is accurate information. In order to become a disciple, you must acquire and master a body of knowledge. So teaching is always part of discipleship.

Jesus was the master Teacher. He taught His twelve disciples the essence of what it means to follow Him. In God's Word we have the body of knowledge God wants us to know.

### THE RIGHT SKILLS

But knowledge alone does not make you a disciple. You also have to know how to take that information and do something with it. Discipleship involves developing your skills. That's why Jesus would teach His disciples, then take them out into situations where they could apply what they were learning.

All of us know brilliant people who have lots of "book sense" but very little common sense. We wonder how these people can be so smart and yet not be able to function well in the situations of daily life.

That's not what a disciple is supposed to be like. A disciple marries the right information with the skill needed to put it

ONE LIFE UNDER GOD

into practice. How important is it we get this picture?

Suppose you need open-heart surgery. The doctor comes into your room the night before the operation and introduces himself. You shake his hand and say, "Doctor, this is a serious thing. How many of these have you done before?"

"You're my first one," he answers.

You reply, "Excuse me?"

"You'll be my first open-heart surgery."

"We need to talk. How do you know you can do this?"

"Well," he replies, "I went to four years of college and to medical school, and I made all A's. In fact, I graduated at the top of my class. I know the parts of the body, and I know the surgical instruments I need to use. You have nothing to worry about."

You are going to say, "Passing tests does not make you a surgeon. I want someone in there who has done this before." And so does every other patient. That's why a medical student does an internship and residency. He has to come alongside someone who has been in surgery before, who knows what to do when complications arise and things happen that aren't covered in the textbook. That new doctor's knowledge is very important, but it's not enough. He needs to be shown how to perform the operation.

That's discipleship. It occurs when a person brings another person or persons along in such a way that the disciple imparts the right information while modeling the right skill.

This is why you cannot be disciples simply by showing up at church on Sunday morning. Worship is an essential component of following Christ. But, like knowledge, it's not the whole picture. Discipleship demands someone walking beside you.

We have an example of disciple making right in our communities: the drug pusher. These guys are slick. They will take a young boy and mold him, giving him the body of information necessary to make a quick dollar, letting him walk beside them as they deal, and then sending him on his own to do what they did.

The issue is not whether you are going to be disciples. The issue is by whom will you be discipled. All of us have people and influences in our lives that shape who we are and what we do. Discipleship demands skills derived from a body of information that is modeled before you.

I want to make three key observations about spiritual growth in becoming a disciple, based on the definition I gave above. These include the process, the movement, and the domain.

## THE PROCESS OF DEVELOPMENT

The first thing you need to know about becoming a disciple is discipleship is a process of spiritual development. I have already quoted Matthew 10:25, but let me give it to you again in context with verse 24: "A disciple is not above his teacher, nor a slave above his master. It is enough for the disciple that he become like his teacher, and the slave like his master."

Matthew 10 is a crucial passage on discipleship, and we'll come back to it again. When Jesus said disciples are to become like their teacher; He was making clear being a disciple is a process.

You do not wake up the day after you are converted and discover you are a spiritual giant, a fully mature disciple. Spiritual growth toward maturity takes time.

This concept reminds me of the story about the farmer who brought his family to the big city for the first time. They were particularly awed by the mall. As the wife toured the stores, the farmer took his son into a bank located in the mall. He saw a very elderly lady enter a room, then a few seconds later a beautiful young woman left the same room. The man looked down at his son and said, "Boy, run and get your mother—fast." Unfortunately we cannot be transformed into disciples in just a few minutes—or a few years, for that matter. It takes time.

But the New Testament does not give us a step-by-step timetable for becoming disciples, nor does it have a list of formal, legalistic steps to be followed. There's a very good reason for this. Although the process of discipleship involves certain basic necessities that are common to all believers, our spiritual experiences are unique to us. Thus Paul admonishes us to work out *our own* salvation—not someone else's—in fear and trembling.

Jesus points out in a picturesque way in Matthew 11:28–30 how you are to go about achieving your own personal spiritual growth: "Come to Me, all who are weary and heavy-laden, and I will give you rest. Take My yoke upon you, and *learn* from Me, for I am gentle and humble in heart; and you will find rest for your souls. For My yoke is easy, and My burden is light."

The word *learn* that we read in this passage is the verb form for the word "disciple." Jesus is saying, "Come and be discipled by Me." This is a wonderful invitation to the process of personal discipleship.

Jesus also paints a vivid picture of what the process looks like when He speaks of His yoke. You have probably seen a horse, a mule, or an ox harnessed around the neck and shoulders in order to pull a wagon or a plow. The yoke is put on for three basic reasons.

One reason for wearing the yoke is to bring the animal under submission, under the control of the one sitting on the wagon or the plow and holding the reins. A yoke makes control possible. In discipleship, Christ is seeking our surrender as we looked at with regard to Romans 12. He wants to bring us under His control.

The yoke also speaks of work to be done. It implies responsibility. God saved you to bring upon you the right kind of responsibility. In other words, when a person yokes something he does it purposefully. There is something he wants to accomplish. God saved you because He has something He wants your life to accomplish. But you can only fulfill the responsibility when you are yoked together with Christ, under His control.

It was a common thing in the ancient world, and still is today in some communities, to train a young ox or mule by yoking it with an older, more experienced animal. That way the young one comes alongside the experienced one to learn how to pull. When the farmer does this he usually adjusts the yoke so most of the weight falls on the experienced animal until the younger one gets the hang of it. When I was a young teenager, my father used to take me with him when he went to preach. He would preach on street corners and give me a fistful of tracts to hand out. Or he would go to a prison to preach and take me with him to witness what he did.

As far as I was concerned, when it was over that was it. I didn't realize then God would later place a call on my life that would necessitate the experiences I had going along with my dad.

When I was in college, I preached on street corners. I preached in prisons. I was the preacher then, but the groundwork of experience was laid for me by my father, who did the work but took me along to show me how it's done.

Jesus says in Matthew 11:28, "If you come unto me and

are weary and heavy-laden, I will give you rest. I will bear the yoke with you, and I will pull the weight" (my own paraphrase).

I said earlier that not every Christian is necessarily a disciple. You can see the difference in verses 28–29. In verse 28 Jesus says, "I will give you rest." But in verse 29 He says, "If you take My yoke, you will find rest" (again, my own paraphrase). What's the difference? Verse 28 is a position. Verse 29 is an experience.

Whenever the Bible talks about rest, it means the enjoyment of God's provision. In other words, as a believer you have God's rest. But you may not be experiencing that rest in your daily life because you have not accepted the yoke. You have peace with God but you may not be enjoying the peace of God. The same can be said of joy, power, and a lot of other blessings.

It's not that these things aren't available to us. The problem is we are not yoked to the One who can give them to us. The yoke implies a different level of commitment. Matthew 11:28 is an invitation to salvation. Verse 29 is an invitation to the fellowship of discipleship.

## THE MOVEMENT TOWARD MATURITY

If discipleship is a process of spiritual development, what's the goal we are developing toward? It's spiritual maturity: becoming a full-grown, well-developed disciple of Jesus Christ.

Paul wrote to the Christians at Corinth, "I, brethren, could not speak to you as to spiritual men, but as to men of flesh, as to infants in Christ" (1 Corinthians 3:1). The biblical term for a mature Christian is "spiritual." Paul expected the Corinthians to be maturing in the faith, but instead they were still acting like spiritual babies.

What's interesting is Paul had gone to Corinth and led these people to Christ about A.D. 50. He was saying, "You should be spiritual by now, but you have not used your time well for spiritual development."

This passage brings up a very simple formula or guideline for spiritual growth: *rate multiplied by the time equals distance.* That is, the rate you grow in your spiritual life in the time you have been allotted determines the distance you will travel down the road of discipleship toward spiritual maturity.

A newborn Christian who dives into the Word and the things of God rather than spending his or her time on other things may burst from the starting blocks and arrive at spiritual maturity faster than a person who has been saved for ten years but is still struggling with the basics of the faith. It's your pace that makes the difference.

By the way, if you really want to pick up your spiritual pace, run with someone who is faster than you, who can set a brisk pace. That's really what discipleship is all about. You cannot run the Christian life alone and run it with any speed or with much real endurance.

The good news is that even though you may have started off slowly, or started fast and then stumbled, you can get back in the race toward spiritual maturity. And I have even better news than that: No matter how you may have messed up, you can still cross the finish line a winner. The issue in the Christian race is not how you start, but how you finish (Hebrews 3:14).

The passage in 1 Corinthians I referred to above is important because it helps you determine how far along you are in your progress toward maturity. In 1 Corinthians 2:14–3:3, Paul identifies four categories of people with respect to the spiritual life.

The first category is the "natural man [who] does not accept the things of the Spirit of God" (2:14). This is the non-Christian, a person living by this world's system who has no capacity to receive spiritual truth. If you realize you are in this category as you read this book, the spiritual necessity for you is to come to Christ and be saved.

But chances are you are already a believer, so one of Paul's next three categories applies to you. The second category is the spiritual man or woman (2:15), the person who "appraises all things, yet he himself is appraised by no one." This is the other end of the spiritual spectrum.

The spiritual person is a mature Christian, a well-developed disciple. The reason that non-Christians can't "appraise" or understand such a person is they don't have the "mind of Christ" (v. 16). But the mind of Christ—the ability to live life from God's perspective, the capacity to think God's thoughts after Him—is available to every true believer.

A mature disciple is one who is able to make divinely informed choices. Paul is saying, "The spiritual person is able to look at, understand, and figure out life from a divine standpoint because he has the mind of Christ."

The third category the apostle identifies in this text is "infants in Christ" (3:1). The baby Christian is someone who is brand new in the faith. Newborn Christians cannot be mature. That's an impossibility. They can be on fire and growing like crazy spiritually, but they cannot be full grown.

Paul's fourth and final category is the "fleshy" or carnal Christian (3:2–3). The difference between a carnal Christian and a baby Christian is the carnal believer has had time to mature. He should know how to live with a heavenly perspective, but instead he thinks and acts like a non-Christian. He makes little progress toward spiritual maturity. This person has not responded to the invitation and challenge to become a disciple.

And lest we think progressing toward mature discipleship is a take-it-or-leave-it deal, let me point you to Hebrews 5:

> About this [Melchizedek] we have much to say, and it is hard to explain, since you have become dull of hear-

ing. For though by this time you ought to be teachers, you need someone to teach you again the basic principles of the oracles of God. You need milk, not solid food. (vv. 11–12 ESV)

The writer of Hebrews had some spiritually nourishing wisdom to teach these believers about the Melchizedek priesthood of Christ, but they had "become dull." Evidently they had been growing, but they were regressing. If you don't go forward you go backward, because there is no such thing as neutrality in the Christian life.

Adults who can't eat solid food are sick. And Christians who still need kindergarten language in order to understand the things of God are not growing. This was the Hebrews' problem, because they had had enough time to be mature.

In fact, the writer says by the time of his letter the Hebrews should have been mature enough to teach and disciple others. Every Christian has been saved to be an influencer—a teacher, a discipler—of another Christian.

But the Hebrews were regressing, so the writer continues in 5:13–14.

For everyone who partakes only of milk is not accustomed to the word of righteousness, for he is an infant. But solid food is for the mature, who because of practice have their senses trained to discern good and evil.

We are supposed to know which way is up spiritually

because we've been trained—which is the word "gymnatized" we talked about earlier. We're supposed to be mature because we've been practicing hard.

It's important to remember that one of the critical elements about the process of spiritual growth is it takes place from the inside out (1 Thessalonians 5:23). As the Holy Spirit empowers the human spirit, the human spirit transforms the soul (personality). The transformed soul then transforms the activity of the body, thus conforming the person's conduct to the image of Christ, which is the essence of discipleship.

For this reason there is such an emphasis on abiding in Christ. As intimacy with Christ is maintained, the transforming process is ignited and enhanced.

## THE RESOURCES FOR OUR GROWTH

God has provided four key resources to help us in this process: (1) Scripture provides the authoritative, objective truth to govern our choices and decision making. 2) The Holy Spirit empowers Christians to accomplish the demands of Scripture as they live under the influence, or full of the Spirit (Ephesians 5:18), which is accomplished as we make worship a lifestyle and not just an event (vv. 19–21). (3) God uses trials to reveal to us our strengths and weaknesses so we can tangibly see the areas that still need work. Trials, while painful, are like a good surgeon's knife, always designed to make us better (James 1:2–5). (4) God gives us relationships so the spiritual passion of others keeps us spiritually hot and the discipleship process is kept on track.

The result of these divine provisions is conformity to the image of Christ. This is demonstrated by the reflection of the fruit of the Spirit in the life of the disciple (Galatians 5:16–25) and a new ability to perceive and understand God's will for our life so we can fulfill His kingdom agenda for us.

The apostle Paul believed spiritual maturity was very achievable to "present every man complete in Christ" (Colossians 1:28).

He believed that in the corporate context of the local church at Colossae each individual member could grow to maturity in Christlikeness. Nothing is said about endless programs, meetings, strategies, and activities that needed to be devised in order to bring about the spiritual development of these disciples. Instead, Scripture gives us a picture of believers coming together to learn about Christ.

I believe this is true not because there is no place in the church for an emphasis on function, but rather because the essence of discipleship is our experience with Jesus Christ. Discipleship, then, is more than the sum total of our religious activities. It is coming to know Christ and having the completeness of His life worked out in us (Colossians 2:9–10).

To be sure, such maturity, while guaranteed, is not automatic. The individual believer bears a responsibility.

## THE DOMAIN OF DISCIPLESHIP

In Colossians 1:13–14 (ESV), the apostle Paul wrote, "He [Christ] has delivered us from the domain of darkness and transferred us to the kingdom of his beloved Son, in whom we have redemption, the forgiveness of sins."

If you are a Christian, God has transferred you to a new domain, a new dominion. You have been placed into a whole new environment, the kingdom of God's beloved Son. You can't be a disciple of the King until you first enter His realm.

John 3 tells the familiar story of Nicodemus, whom we might call a model person. He was a Jewish Pharisee, but he had a Greek name. In that culture, giving a Jewish boy a Greek name meant his parents were high society, "tall cotton," well cultured.

So Nicodemus had culture and wealth. As a Pharisee, he was also at the top of the pile religiously. Nicodemus had it all, but Jesus said, "You must be born again" (John 3:7).

Getting into God's kingdom has nothing to do with what side of town you live on or how often you go to church. It requires a new spiritual birth. That's the only way you get a passport to the kingdom. This spiritual rebirth only comes from placing your faith in Jesus Christ alone as your personal Sin-Bearer because of His substitutionary death on the cross and His victorious resurrection from the dead (Romans 10:9–10).

When I travel, I have a passport that gives me access to other nations. If you have been born "from above" (a better translation than "again") by personal faith in the finished work of Jesus Christ, your sins are forgiven and God has given you a passport into His kingdom.

That passport is the blood of Jesus, and it gets you into His domain. What's it like there? Romans 14:17 says the kingdom of God is not food and drink but "righteousness and peace and joy in the Holy Spirit." It's a spiritual realm.

Paul says we are now citizens of another kingdom, which is owned by another King (Philippians 3:20; 1 Timothy 1:17). Our first obligation is not to this world system that leaves God out. Our first obligation and allegiance is to the kingdom of God.

Several years ago everybody was singing, "I'm proud to be an American." When we go to ball games we stand up and sing the national anthem, giving honor to our country. We do so because we are Americans.

What would people say about an American who announces, "I am not going to sing that song or honor that flag"? Most people would say that person needs to move on to another country. We do so because we are Americans.

Every day when you and I wake up we should say, "I pledge allegiance to Christ and to the cross He died on to forgive my sin." We owe our allegiance to the kingdom of God. That's why we are trying to learn His kingdom agenda.

Is it possible for believers to miss the kingdom in their personal spiritual growth? It is—not in terms of salvation but in terms of discipleship.

How does it happen? It happens when we become busy trying to be entertained by the world instead of setting our eyes on Christ.

Anyone who knows me can tell you I like amusement parks with their wild rides and all of that. At the huge state fair of Texas, they have those crazy sideshows featuring all manner of oddities. We used to visit them when the kids were small.

But I don't go to the sideshows anymore for a simple reason: they aren't worth the price of admission. They use mirrors to make that alligator look huge, and the so-called "half man, half animal" is just a man dressed up in a crazy outfit.

That's what the world's system is like. It will promise you a great sideshow, but after you have taken a peek you realize it isn't what was advertised. The Bible says: "Do not love the world nor the things in the world. If anyone loves the world, the love of the Father is not in him. For all that is in the world, the lust of the flesh and the lust of the eyes and the boastful pride of life, is not from the Father, but is from the world" (1 John 2:15–16).

The world will give you a sideshow, but it won't give you life or purpose or direction because you belong to a different realm, a spiritual nation.

## COME TO THE KINGDOM

You may say, "Tony, I'm a Christian, but I don't have a sense I am living in this spiritual domain." Perhaps that's because you have not fully committed yourself to your new domain.

A man once became lost in the desert. His throat was parched, and he knew he wouldn't live much longer if he didn't get some water.

Off in the distance he saw a little old shack. He made his way to the shack and found a pump inside with a jug of water sitting next to it. He reached for the jug to take a drink, only to find this note on the jug: "The pump will give you all the water you need. But in order to prime the pump, you must pour in all the water in the jug."

This man had a dilemma. Should he drink the water in the jug and be out of water and perhaps be unable to get more, or should he believe the note and use the water he had to prime the pump?

He began to think through his choices. "Suppose I pour all my water in the pump and nothing happens? I not only lose the water—I may lose my life.

"On the other hand, if there is a well underneath this pump and I use the water to prime it, then I can get all the water I need."

This thirsty man's dilemma is the question we have to ask ourselves as disciples. Do we get all we can now because there might not be much later? Or do we give up what we can get now because of all that's available if we are willing to take the risk of committing ourselves to Christ?

The man thought for a moment and decided to take the risk. He poured the contents of the jug into the pump and began to work the handle. Sweat broke out on his forehead, as nothing happened at first.

But as he pumped, a few drops of water appeared, and then came a huge gush. He drank all he wanted, took a bath, then filled up every other container he could find in the shack.

Because he was willing to give up momentary satisfaction, the man got all the water he needed. Now the note also said, "After you have finished, please refill the jug for the next traveler." The man refilled the jug and then added to the note, "Please prime the pump. Believe me, it works."

We need to prime the pump. Some of us are half-stepping on Christ. We're trying to live in two worlds at the same time. We want to be sacred and secular, worldly and spiritual. We want to love God and love this world order. But my charge to you to remember is this: you can have the world if you want it—you just can't have the world *and* God.

You have to pour in all the water—give God everything you have—if you want God to pour His covenantal blessings back on you. Only in the domain of the kingdom will you discover God's abundance and power to experience personal victory in your life.

# CHAPTER THREE

# YOUR PURPOSE AND YOUR CALLING

Maybe you have heard the story about the man who once said he was dying to finish high school so he could go to college. But when he got to college, he said he was dying to finish college so he could start his career. Then when he got to his career, he said he was dying to finish his career so he could start his retirement. And now that he's in his retirement he has discovered he has gotten so old that he is just plain dying, having never gotten around to truly living.

Many Christians today are living life in falsetto—just out of range. Maybe you are one of them: where it seems that your get-up-and-go has gotten-up-and-gone. A sense of purpose somehow has eluded you. Rather than your life encapsulating the brilliance of the noonday sun, it has become more like a flicker of a candle—all of the brilliance has gone.

People will spend their entire lives trying to climb the ladder of success only to discover once they reach the top that the ladder was leaning against the wrong wall. And the top of the ladder isn't all it was cracked up to be. A sense of emptiness, purposelessness, and even meandering nags at many people today. That's one reason why many men like to wear jerseys with other men's names and numbers on them—simply because they have not discovered how to both own and fulfill the purpose of their own name and number as a kingdom man. They lack their own sense of substance, significance, dignity, greatness, and reason for being.

Yet God is a God of purpose. All throughout Scripture God does what He does because He has a reason for doing it. He is a King over an intentional kingdom. As a follower of His and a subject in His kingdom, you are also a person of purpose. You have not been placed on earth simply to meander through the months and many moons of your lifetime.

Too many of us merely exist rather than live as if we are called. We work for a living but never get around to working for a life. We suffer from what I call the "same ol' same" disease.

Does this ever sound like you? Every morning you get up out of that same ol' bed. You go to that same ol' bathroom and look in that same ol' mirror at that same ol' face. You go to that same ol' closet to choose from those same ol' clothes.

Then you go to that same ol' table to eat that same ol' breakfast. You get up and walk to that same ol' garage, get in that same ol' car, head down that same ol' road to arrive at that same ol' job. There you do that same ol' work for that same ol' pay.

At the end of the day you head back down that same ol' road, pull into that same ol' garage, and walk into that same ol' house. You sit down in that same ol' chair to watch those same ol' programs on that same ol' television. Or you surf that same ol' Internet.

At dinnertime, you pull up to that same ol' table and eat that same ol' dinner again from those same ol' dishes. Then you fall into that same ol' bed so you can wake up the next day and start that same ol' routine again.

Where is the sense of purpose in a life like that? Where is the sense that, when you go to bed tonight, you are going to wake up tomorrow on the next leg of an epic adventure far greater than anything you could have ever scripted yourself?

Friend, that epic adventure is the kingdom of God. The journey comes when you are pursuing His kingdom agenda. If you settle for anything less, you miss God's reason for redeeming you and positioning you here on earth.

Do you ever feel you could use a little bit of caffeine in your Christian cup? What you are lacking is clarity on your calling. Because when you live out your purpose—when you are fulfilling your destiny—you are experiencing God's energizing and eternally significant power in your life while leveraging and maximizing your life's fullest potential.

Your calling is *the customized life purpose God has ordained and equipped you to accomplish in order to bring Him the greatest glory and achieve the maximum expansion of His kingdom.*

You may want to review that definition a time or two before reading on. It is foundational to everything we are going to talk about in this chapter.

A divine calling always has to do with God's glory, with fulfilling His kingdom agenda. It involves the display of who you are in such a way that puts God's kingdom in full view for others to see. For example, a popular store in New York City is Saks Fifth Avenue. Outside of Saks are windows that line the streets so passersby can catch a glimpse of what is inside this so-called kingdom called Saks. The owners make a major investment in the mannequins and display items in these windows to showcase to the outside world what their kingdom has to offer.

As a child of the King, God has invested His image in you and placed you on display. You are to reflect Him and His kingdom through your personalized purpose and calling in such a remarkable fashion that people want to know more about the kingdom you represent. That is your destiny, which also means if you and I are not advancing God's kingdom and bringing Him glory, we have not yet found our calling. Let's look at several aspects of a calling that will help to flesh out this definition.

## A CUSTOMIZED LIFE PURPOSE

First, God's calling in your life is customized. It is uniquely designed to help you reflect God's purpose for your life. This is why everyone must "work out" his or her own salvation (Philippians 2:12). Keep in mind you are the only you that will ever exist. There will never be another just like you. You are not off the rack—you are custom made, rare, and special.

Nobody has your specific calling but you. Once you realize that, you will realize you do not need to try and be someone else. Why would you want to be someone else anyhow? God already has one of them. If you become one of them, God doesn't have one of you. What's more, you will never feel more alive than when you are carrying out the destiny specifically designed for you.

Friend, if you do not pursue and live out your calling, you will spend your entire life wishing you were someone else. You will spend your entire life trying to be someone that you are not. If you are not happy with who you are, it is because you have not yet discovered who you *are*.

Just like your fingerprints and your DNA are uniquely

yours, your calling is uniquely yours. That truth ought to have an impact on how you view and respond to what is going on around you.

One of the reasons people can't find their calling is they are trying to tell themselves why they have been called. They are trying to self-define their own calling. But keep in mind a calling always assumes a caller. If your phone is ringing, someone is calling you. You are not calling yourself.

One of the foundational steps to living out your calling is understanding God is the caller and you are the callee. God is the manufacturer. You are the design. God is the creator. You are the created. So you can never discover your destiny apart from God. It is impossible.

The biblical character who best exemplifies this is Moses. For starters, Moses fled from Egypt after killing an Egyptian (Exodus 2:11–15). God would call Moses to lead Israel out of Egypt (Exodus 3), but for forty years Moses had settled for being a shepherd. He had made some mistakes, he had failed, and he had settled for hanging out with sheep on the backside of a desert.

Moses was what most would consider to be an ordinary believer.

So here he was, leading the sheep of his father-in-law, Jethro. He came to Horeb, "the mountain of God" (Exodus 3:1) and there he encountered God:

The angel of the LORD appeared to him in a blazing fire from the midst of a bush; and he looked, and behold, the bush was burning with fire, yet the bush was not consumed. So Moses said, "I must turn aside now, and see this marvelous sight, why the bush is not burned up." When the LORD saw that he turned aside to look, God called to him from the midst of the bush, and said, "Moses, Moses!" And he said, "Here I am." (3:2–4)

If you want to know your calling, don't go "calling-looking." Go God-looking. God knows where He wants you, what He is calling you to do, when He wants you to do it, and how He wants it done. Therefore, if you want to find your calling, look for God. When you find God, His calling will find you.

God's calling for your life will be experienced out of your relationship with Him. If there is no relationship, you will not know what your calling is all about.

Moses met God at a burning bush because he came to the mountain where God was hanging out. Now Moses didn't know he was going to meet God that day, but he was in God's presence.

If you want to know your calling, you have to go where God is. If you never have time to go before the face of God, you won't find your calling. If you never have time to spend in God's Word, you won't find your calling. If you never have time to be around the people of God, you will never find your calling.

We spend so much time doing things that may be OK within themselves but rob us of time in God's presence. When you encounter God, He will lead you to your calling. Your calling finds you when you find God.

I can attest to that. As a young man I was frequently preoccupied with playing football. As a teenager, I thought football was the sole purpose for living. Yet God continued to call out to me and draw me close to Him through my parents' godly examples, church, and the nearly constant playing of Bible teachers my father would have playing on the radio at home. It was in the midst of serving God alongside my father I began to take steps to know God more intimately for myself.

On one particular evening God located me at an evangelistic crusade when B. Sam Hart had come to a nearby town. The next thing I knew I was there under the tent asking God, "What do You want me to do for You with the rest of my life?"

I was already a Christian and serving God here and there, but my main focus was still on me and my desire to play football. When God found me that day and called me into His service, He set into motion a series of events that would detour me radically from the direction I wanted to go. My calling found me because I was in God's presence.

At the burning bush, Moses saw God in a unique way. It

was an ordinary bush, but it wasn't an ordinary day. When God shows up, any old bush will do because when God shows up, He turns the ordinary into the extraordinary. That's the essence of a calling—when God shows up in your life in an extraordinary way.

When I was under that tent, it was as if nobody else was under that tent but God and me. It was like God called my name and singled me out. I knew that day God was calling me into His service for the remainder of my time on earth, and I have never looked back.

It was just an ordinary tent and an ordinary day, but it was an extraordinary moment in my life. I heard God's call because I was listening to His Word.

## THE PERSON BEFORE THE CALLING

God was about to give Moses his calling. But Moses did not get God's program until he responded to God's Person. The person precedes the program. Relationship precedes the calling.

It's not enough to get on your knees and say, "Lord, show me my calling; show me Your program," when your relationship with Him is in disrepair. If you don't relate to His Person, God won't trust you with His program.

Have you ever tried to go out on a date with your spouse when the two of you aren't getting along? You are in for a miserable evening trying to accomplish a program when the relationship is ruptured. When the relationship is repaired, the program is a lot easier and a lot sweeter. God doesn't want you showing up only when you want something from Him. He wants an ongoing relationship with you.

Luke 10:38–42 is a textbook example of what I'm talking about. It's the story of Martha and Mary and a dinner for Jesus.

Martha had a program to accomplish. She was cooking dinner for Jesus and the apostles—twelve preachers and her Lord. And she was getting upset because Mary was more interested in the person. She was sitting at Jesus' feet.

So here's Martha, cooking fried chicken—the gospel bird—for these preachers. Sweat is running down her face, and Mary is nowhere to be found. Martha goes and looks in the den, and there is Mary sitting at Jesus' feet.

Martha became irritated and complained, "Lord, do You not care that my sister has left me to do all the serving alone? Then tell her to help me [because I'm not talking to her right now]" (my paraphrase of v. 40).

Jesus said, "Martha, Martha."

Watch out whenever Jesus calls your name twice! He said, "Martha, Martha, you are worried and bothered about so many things; but only one thing is necessary, for Mary has chosen the good part, which shall not be taken away from her" (Luke 10:41–42).

Jesus was saying, "Martha, a casserole will do. Just cook one dish; then come sit at My feet. Mary has chosen to make Me more important than your cooking program. She is better off out here with Me than you are there in the kitchen."

Jesus knew if He sent Mary into the kitchen with Martha He would have two frustrated women on His hands. But if Mary stayed with Him, He would have somebody whose life was focused on Him.

I'll say it again. God wants a relationship with you before He is willing to give you His program.

## A PERSONALIZED COMMITMENT

Once you get the Person ahead of the program, you get a personalized calling. Notice back in Exodus 3 that Jesus called Moses by name. Moses' call came out of a personal commitment. Two of my favorite verses in the Bible are about this kind of commitment, and they're found in Romans 12:1–2:

> Therefore, I urge you, brethren, by the mercies of God, to present your bodies a living and holy sacrifice, acceptable to God, which is your spiritual service of worship. And do not be conformed to this world, but be transformed by the renewing of your mind, so that you may prove what the will of God is, that which is good and acceptable and perfect.

These verses are saying the same thing we have been talking about. Paul said if you are going to know God's will for your life, your calling in the kingdom, God must own all of you.

God is not impressed with a two-hour visit on Sunday. He wants to own your life. He wants to be in charge.

Paul said, "Present your bodies a living . . . sacrifice." That's an oxymoron; sacrifices were put to death. How can you be a living dead thing?

Paul explained it in another of my favorite verses,

> "I have been crucified with Christ; and it is no longer I who live, but Christ lives in me; and the life which I now live in the flesh I live by faith in the Son of God, who loved me, and gave Himself up for me." (Galatians 2:20)

Paul considered himself a living dead person, because he was dead to his own life and his plans and alive to God's. So if you asked, "Paul, what are your dreams?" he would say, "I don't know. Dead people don't dream."

"Paul, what are your goals?"

"I don't know. Dead people don't set goals."

"Paul, what about your future?"

"Dead people don't have a future."

But if you changed the question and asked, "Paul, what

about God's goal for you?" he would say, "We can talk about that!" Paul had defined the totality of his life through his commitment to Jesus Christ. That's why you couldn't intimidate him.

People came to Paul one day and said, "Paul, we are going to kill you."

He answered, "That's cool. For me, to die is gain."

"All right, we're going to let you live."

"That's cool too. For me, to live is Christ."

"Well, since you're so cool about everything, we are going to beat you and make you suffer."

"That's also cool, because I consider that the sufferings of this present time are not worthy to be compared with the glory that is to be revealed in us" (Romans 8:18; Philippians 1:21). You couldn't intimidate him. It didn't matter to Paul what happened. It was all Christ to him.

## THE CERTAINTY OF YOUR CALLING

Why does God want the totality of your life before He shows you your calling?

We have an answer in John 7:16–17, where Jesus said, "My teaching is not Mine, but His who sent Me. If anyone is willing to do His will, he will know of the teaching, whether it is of God or whether I speak from Myself."

You must be willing to do God's will before you know His

will. Many of us say to God, "Show me what You want me to do, and I will let You know whether I am into that or not. Let me know the plan, and I will tell You whether I plan to do it."

No, no. God's plan is not up for negotiation. God is only going to reveal your calling to you when you are committed to doing it ahead of time. God will not negotiate His will.

As Romans 12:1–2 says, you must give all of yourself to God and none of yourself to the world system that wants independence from God.

God says if we conform to this world, He will not reveal His calling for our lives. We must say, as Moses said to God at the burning bush, "Here I am" (Exodus 3:4). In other words, "What do You want of me, Lord? I am ready to obey."

In Mark 8:34–36, Jesus made one of the most profound statements in all of Scripture:

> If anyone wishes to come after Me, he must deny himself, and take up his cross and follow Me. For whoever wishes to save his life will lose it; but whoever loses his life for My sake and the gospel's will save it. For what does it profit a man to gain the whole world, and forfeit his soul?

We have already talked about what it means to deny yourself and carry your cross. Here, Jesus adds the teaching about saving and losing your life.

How do you save your life yet lose it? By going after the world. When you do that you forfeit your life, because life consists of more than the stuff you accumulate.

Many people have a house but no longer have a home. Many people have money but don't have peace. Many people have plans but don't have any purpose. This principle of saving and losing your life is fixed. It's another way of saying you can't find God's calling for your life when you're busy trying to save it by gaining the world.

Giving yourself totally to God is giving Him full power over your life. When you do, you experience the abundant life He has promised to give you. When I committed my life to God's calling for me at the age of eighteen, I had no idea what God had in mind.

All I knew was, "Whatever You want me to do, Lord, however You want me to do it, wherever You want it done, I am Yours." Then the Holy Spirit took over, and God began unfolding a series of events that has brought me to this point.

Jesus says the way to find your life is to lose it for His sake. When you do that, God will reveal your calling to you, and the puzzle of life will begin to come together.

My oldest daughter, Chrystal, was a puzzle fanatic when she was younger. She was always putting puzzles together. One day I brought home a one-thousand-piece puzzle. Chrystal was excited.

She took the puzzle, went to her room, but came back a

couple of hours later looking very upset. "Daddy, why did you buy me this puzzle? It has too many pieces!"

Life is like that. It has too many pieces. If you try to put them together by yourself, you will only frustrate yourself. It you want to put the pieces of your life together, God must own you. He is the One who holds the finished image of your calling. Putting together a puzzle without seeing the image of the final product is nearly impossible. Look to Him because He knows where He is taking you.

In fact, many Christians are living their lives with a feeling of insignificance because they cannot see how they relate to the much larger, comprehensive puzzle called God's purpose. You may be a fancy piece, pretty piece, handsome piece, or well-crafted piece, but until you connect to the greater meaning for which you were created, you are just a piece without a picture.

The picture God has created us all to form is the maximizing of His glory and the expansion of His kingdom through the impact of your good works. Good works can be defined as *biblically authorized activities that benefit people for time and eternity, for which God gets the credit.* If you are a Christian, whatever you are called to do will achieve both of those things. God's kingdom is His comprehensive rule over creation. To be involved in fulfilling your destiny means the presence of God is being manifested to a greater degree because of what you do.

Every Christian is part of God's kingdom and has a piece to play in God's overarching puzzle called life. To advance God's kingdom isn't solely for professional ministers or evangelists. It is for everyone. As a child of the King, you have been rescued "from the domain of darkness, and transferred . . . to the kingdom of His beloved Son" (Colossians 1:13). That means everything you do has become kingdom activity, even if what you are doing is considered secular activity. There is no distinction any longer between secular and sacred when you are a kingdom-minded person, because everything is sacred when it comes under the overarching rule of the King in His kingdom.

If you are a mother and you are washing dishes for your family, you wash them sacredly. If you are a computer programmer and you are programming for your company, you do your programming sacredly. "Whether, then, you eat or drink or whatever you do, do all to the glory of God" (1 Corinthians 10:31).

But you may say, "It's too late for me to find God's calling, Tony. I've already made too many mistakes."

Well, Moses was a murderer. I doubt if you've ever killed anyone, yet God still met Moses at the burning bush. God transformed Moses and called him into His service to accomplish His will.

So how do you get started finding and fulfilling your calling?

## WORK OUT YOUR SALVATION

First, you are to work out your own salvation. Philippians 2:12–13 is another of those seminal passages for understanding the call of God on your life. Paul wrote, "Work out your salvation with fear and trembling; for it is God who is at work in you, both to will and to work for His good pleasure."

Notice you have something to do in discerning God's call. You can't live off what your mother did for the Lord. You can't make it on your father's faith. You need to find the calling of God for your life.

Others can certainly help you in the process. Get all the information you can. But then you need to go on your face before God, asking Him to show you what He wants you to do. You cannot piggyback on another believer to find your calling.

## GOD AT WORK IN YOU

Notice what else Paul said here. Your work will not be in vain because God is also at work in you.

Paul was not talking about working to become a Christian. You can't work to become a Christian. But once you are saved by the grace of God, He works in you in order to work through you.

So you are at work, and God is at work. Your responsibility

is to commit yourself to God and seek His will.

You don't just wake up one morning and find your calling. You have to go through the process, but God meets you there.

## THE NEED TO RESPOND

Let's go back to Moses. He has seen an extraordinary sight: A bush is burning, yet it is not consumed.

Read Exodus 3:3–4 again and you'll notice when Moses stopped to look at the bush God called to him. God didn't call him until Moses responded.

If you don't respond to what God shows you, He won't show you any more. If you don't respond to the little light He gives you, don't ask for a lot of light.

One day I gave my younger son, Jonathan, three dollars for lunch money. He lost it, so he came to me and said, "Daddy, I need five dollars for lunch."

There was something wrong here. I had given him three dollars, and he had lost it. But instead of asking me for three dollars again, he wanted five dollars. He wanted back the money that he lost—and more.

You cannot waste what God gives you and then ask Him for more. Many of us go before the face of God wanting big stuff when we have not yet said yes to the little things He has commanded us to do.

God won't be used that way. If God cannot trust us to

respond correctly with what He gives us, we don't need to be asking Him for more.

We pray, "Lord, lead me in my career; show me the calling You have for me. Give me direction in my life."

God's response is, "Are you willing to look at the bush?"

The biblical principle is this: "Whoever has, to him shall more be given; and whoever does not have, even what he thinks he has shall be taken away from him" (Luke 8:18). That's what Jesus said.

So do not shun God when He speaks to your heart, because He is preparing to take you to the next level.

Moses responded, and then he heard the call. God's voice came from the midst of the bush, "Do not come near here; remove your sandals from your feet, for the place on which you are standing is holy ground" (Exodus 3:5).

Why did Moses have to take off his sandals? Because when you are standing in the presence of God, even a quarter-inch of leather is too high. When you come into His presence, you go as low as you possibly can.

God demands humility if He is going to show you your calling in His kingdom. As long as you can do it all by yourself, you don't need God. And if you don't need God it can't be His calling, because God's calling on your life will always be greater than anything you could ever accomplish on your own.

God wants you to acknowledge this and come before Him humbly. When you approach Him with your spiritual shoes off, admitting you have no reason to be elevated in His sight, God will speak to you. He will lead you into your destiny, the purpose He has divinely ordained for your life.

Let me show you how Moses' forty years of learning humility in the desert changed things for him when it came to God's calling. As Moses stood before the bush, God told him, in essence, "I am going to deliver My people Israel from Egypt, and I am sending you to Pharaoh to be their deliverer" (see Exodus 3:7–10).

Moses' response was, "Who am I, that I should go to Pharaoh, and that I should bring the sons of Israel out of Egypt?" (v. 11).

Forty years earlier, Moses would have said, "You got it, Lord. Pharaoh doesn't know who he is dealing with. I am the man. I'm going to go and take God along with me, and we're going to wipe out Pharaoh." But Moses had been humbled. Now he wasn't so sure of himself.

Let me tell you a secret. God will do whatever it takes to humble you and me, even if it hurts. This is because God hates nothing more than pride. So Moses, the formerly proud man, said, "Who, me?"

Now we have a small problem. Moses has humbled himself, he has responded to God, and God has revealed Moses' calling to him.

But Moses is overwhelmed by what God is asking him to do, and he begins to back off. He feels inadequate. In Exodus

3:13 Moses asks, "I am going to the sons of Israel, and I will say to them, 'The God of your fathers has sent me to you.' Now they may say to me, 'What is His name?' What shall I say to them?"

## A POWERFUL PROVISION

What a great answer God gave Moses: "'I AM WHO I AM'; and He said, 'Thus you shall say to the sons of Israel, "I AM has sent me to you"'" (v. 14).

That's a very powerful phrase. "I AM WHO I AM" is the personal name of God, the one we transliterate as Yahweh. Notice the name is in the present tense. This is the personal God who is ever in the present tense.

Now, whenever you or I say, "I am," that only covers today. If we were talking about yesterday, we would have to say, "I was." And if we were talking about tomorrow, we would have to say, "I will be."

But not God. He is never "I was," or "I will be." He is "I AM." God has no past, no beginning. And He has no future, no ending. Everything is in the eternal present with Him.

This name means God is self-existent and self-sufficient. When God wants help, He looks to Himself. When God wants praise, He looks to Himself. He invites us to praise Him, but He doesn't need it. When God wants to do something, He looks to Himself. He is the great I AM.

God is saying to Moses, "You can fulfill your calling because I AM your sufficiency. I AM whatever you need. If you need a miracle, I AM your miracle. If you need help, I AM your help. If you need power, I AM your power. If you need strength, I AM your strength. I AM whatever you need."

Moses is in good company here. The Bible is full of stories of men and women who were called by God to do difficult and even impossible things and found the great I AM to be sufficient.

The patriarch Joseph was called. But his calling didn't mean an easy life. He was sold into slavery in Egypt by his brothers. He was falsely accused by the wife of his Egyptian master. He was thrown into jail and languished there for years.

But if Joseph were here today, he would repeat the testimony he gave his brothers in Genesis 50:20: "You meant evil against me, but God meant it for good." God empowered Joseph to fulfill his calling, which ultimately was to save his family from death.

If John Mark were here, he would tell you about God's sufficiency to fulfill his calling. John Mark went out with Paul as an associate in the ministry, but he pulled a Benedict Arnold. He quit and went home when the going got tough.

Paul said, "I can't use John Mark anymore. He might go left on me." But Barnabas stepped in and gave John Mark another chance to do God's work (Acts 15:36–40). And even though John Mark had messed up, he found grace from the

Lord and became a valuable worker—even to Paul (2 Timothy 4:11).

John Mark—we know him just as Mark—got a second chance on his calling, and he made good on it. So good there's a book in the Bible that bears his name.

The apostle Peter was called, but he denied the Lord three times. He had to get "recalled" three times into God's service (John 21:15–17), and that time he didn't fail.

The biblical story of Esther is about a beautiful woman. God used Esther's beauty and her background to accomplish His destiny for her life. Because of her beauty, Esther was chosen by King Ahasuerus as his new bride. Yet once she moved into the big house and got used to the money, cars, clothes, and lifestyle, a plot was made to bring about a genocide on her people. Apparently Esther had gotten so used to her new way of life she didn't feel like risking it in order to help her people.

This is when Esther's uncle, Mordecai, had to remind her of her purpose. He said, "Do not imagine that you in the king's palace can escape any more than all the Jews. For if you remain silent at this time, relief and deliverance will arise for the Jews from another place and you and your father's house will perish. And who knows whether you have not attained royalty for such a time as this?" (Esther 4:13, 14).

In other words, "Esther, moving uptown had a purpose. It wasn't just about getting you out of the hood. Being pretty had a purpose. It wasn't just about you falling in love. God put you in a strategic position at a strategic time to fulfill a strategic purpose that reached beyond just shopping and customizing your wardrobe."

Esther was to look at her life in terms of her calling, not merely in terms of her money, status, image, house, and relationships. She was to view it in terms of her reason for being in connection with God's kingdom and His agenda.

A person who is serious about fulfilling the reason why they have been placed on earth will learn to view all of life through the grid of God's intentions. That worldview will then impact their decisions.

## IT'S GOD'S CALL

If you know Jesus Christ as Savior, God has a calling for you today.

You say, "But I don't know what my calling is." That's all right. Go to the Caller and tell Him you're ready to be the callee, and He will reveal your calling when it is time for you to know it. It's His call, after all.

The story is told that legendary baseball umpire Bill Klem was working behind home plate one day when a runner came sliding into home amidst a huge cloud of dust. The catcher slapped the tag on the runner, and Klem jumped up to make the call.

But Klem hesitated for a second, and everyone started yelling. The runner and his team started shouting he was safe. The catcher and his team screamed that the runner was out. The players all crowded around Klem yelling, "Safe!" "Out!" "Safe!" "Out!"

Klem, who was known for running a game with an iron hand, growled back, "He ain't nothing until I say what he is!"

Bill Klem was right. The call belongs to the one who is in charge. Your responsibility is to be available to God when He wants to call you. As you trust in Him instead of your own understanding (Proverbs 3:5), He will show you step-by-step, moment by moment, what you are supposed to do and where you are supposed to do it.

I don't know what God has called you to do. But I know He wants you to come to Him and say, "Whatever You call me to do, I will do. You make the call." Do that, and then hang on for an epic adventure of power, purpose, and peace.

One of the most noted catchers of all time was Yogi Berra. Yogi was a catcher for the New York Yankees. One day Yogi was taunting equally legendary player Hank Aaron who played for the Atlanta Braves. When Hank came up to bat, Yogi tried to distract him. He told Hank he would do better as a ballplayer if he would hold the bat right. "You're supposed to hold the bat so that you're looking at the trademark. You're holding it wrong," Yogi said.

On the very next pitch, Hank hit the ball into the left-field bleachers. Hank rounded the bases and when he came into home plate with Yogi standing there staring at him with his mask in hand, he took one look at Yogi and replied, "I didn't come here to read."

Friend, when you know your customized life calling, other people can no longer throw you off track. Circumstances can no longer deter you. Rather than striking out at the home plate of life, you will fulfill the reason God has positioned you in His kingdom. You will circle all of the bases before you reach your final Home.

CHAPTER FOUR

# RENEWING YOUR MIND

One disease becomes more unsettling to me every time I hear about it—Alzheimer's. Somehow this disease causes the mind to deteriorate in such a way that the victim loses the power to think clearly and control what he or she does.

Alzheimer's sufferers become incapacitated. They lose their ability to remember and recognize familiar people and things. As the disease advances, the victim's mind loses the ability to tell the body what to do and how to function.

So the person who develops Alzheimer's is at the mercy of another person. Someone else must feed and clothe and lead the patient. One reason Alzheimer's is so terrible is it tends to have a dehumanizing effect on its victims. The reality is when the mind goes, virtually everything else goes with it.

A lot of believers are suffering from spiritual Alzheimer's. This malady manifests itself in a deterioration of the proper application of the mind of Christ—what I would like to call a kingdom mind—that should be operating in every believer's life. The result is a life that is no longer under Christ's control.

A Christian who suffers from spiritual Alzheimer's loses the ability to apply a spiritual mind to his or her daily life. He or she forgets how to think in terms of a kingdom agenda. He or she develops a worldly mind, and when someone has a worldly mind they will do worldly things and develop worldly habits.

We need to talk about the mind in relation to God's kingdom agenda, because if we can get our minds working properly our souls and bodies will follow suit.

Your greatest problem, and mine, is not what we do. Our greatest problem is the way we think. In order to transform what we do, we must first transform how we think. In the words of the writer of Proverbs, "As [a person] thinks within himself, so he is" (Proverbs 23:7).

The mind is the key to our entire being, which is why the great challenge for us today is to develop a kingdom mentality: a way of thinking that is in concert with the kingdom of which we have become a part.

## THE NECESSITY OF A KINGDOM MIND

The first thing we need to understand is the necessity of having a kingdom mind.

I want to begin by looking at Isaiah 55:8. It is very relevant to our topic here, so I'll give it to you again: "'My thoughts are not your thoughts, nor are your ways My ways,' declares the Lord." How far apart are the two? As far as heaven is from earth (see v. 9)!

Because God is transcendent and distinct from His creation, His way of approaching and analyzing an issue is not going to be your way.

That's why you need to develop the mind of the King. You need a kingdom mentality, a kingdom way of thinking, so you can get God's mind on the issues of your life. Whether we are talking about marriage, sex, money, children, or any other issue, God's thinking on the subject will be different than the way this world thinks about it.

Your ability and your decision to develop a kingdom mind will also determine whether you taste victory or defeat in your daily spiritual life. Paul wrote in Romans 8:

> Those who are according to the flesh set their minds
> on the things of the flesh, but those who are according
> to the Spirit, the things of the Spirit. For the mind set
> on the flesh is death, but the mind set on the Spirit

is life and peace, because the mind set on the flesh is hostile toward God; for it does not subject itself to the law of God, for it is not even able to do so. (vv. 5–7)

Where you set your mind will determine whether you have victory or defeat in life. What you sow in your mind will come out through your mouth, your hands, and your feet. The body will express what is in the mind.

That's why we need to begin by dealing with the way we think. If we can transform our thoughts and bring our minds under the authority of Christ, we have laid the foundation for transforming our actions.

## THE KEY TO GOD'S WILL

When you develop a kingdom mind you will begin experiencing God's will for your life. This is because God reveals His will to our minds.

If you want to know God's will, you need to give God your mind. He must be able to control your thoughts. The mind is to the soul what the brain is to the body—the control center. So if I am acting like a fool, it's because I'm thinking like a fool. The same is true if I am acting ignorantly. And if I am acting "kingdomly," carrying out a kingdom agenda, it's because I am thinking with a kingdom mind.

When Lois and I first met, she didn't like me that much.

But I saw her and liked her. Besides, she was cooking fried chicken that day. So I thought we had a very, very good start!

But she didn't like me. I was trying to talk to her, and she wouldn't halfway talk. She was acting hard to get and all that kind of stuff. But she didn't know who she was messing with! I knew I had to get into her mind.

So I pulled out all that ancient rap I knew from the streets of Baltimore, and I poured it on Lois. I was rapping and trying to charm her and just making up all kinds of stuff.

I remember one time we went for a walk near Lois's house and stood at a seawall with the ocean slapping up against it. It was evening, and the stars were out. I was naming stars, making up constellations, just rappin' to try to impress Lois. I remember pointing to one star and saying, "That star is probably sitting over my hometown of Baltimore, Maryland, right now."

I should be embarrassed to tell you all of this! I had no idea what I was talking about. But despite that, my relationship with Lois went from her thinking "I don't like him" to "He's all right." So I messed with her mind a little bit more.

Then we moved from "He's all right" to "He's not that bad." The next stage was "I kind of like him." Then it was "I am in love with him," and from there it was "I've got to have him." When I got her mind, I got her, and she's been by my side ever since.

My point is when you change the mind, you can change

the emotions and the actions.

So if you really want to think like God thinks, to live in victory, and to know God's will, fix your mind first. A kingdom mind is indispensable to a kingdom life.

## THE NATURE OF A KINGDOM MIND

Next let's discover the nature of a mind that operates by a kingdom mentality:

> Things which eye has not seen and ear has not heard,
> And which have not entered the heart of man,
> All that God has prepared for those who love Him.
> For to us God revealed them through the Spirit . . .
> For who among men knows the thoughts of a man
> except the spirit of the man, which is in him? Even so
> the thoughts of God no one knows except the Spirit of
> God. (1 Corinthians 2:9–11)

Here's the first thing Paul said about a kingdom mind. It can grasp things outside the normal limitations of the human senses because it is illuminated by God's Spirit. God can deal with kingdom-thinking people in realms beyond what the eyes can see and the ears can hear.

In fact, when God takes possession of your mind the way He wants to and gives you a kingdom mentality, He can reveal stuff to you that would never enter a human mind left to itself.

All the good things God has prepared for us in this life are beyond our senses. His kingdom agenda reaches beyond what we can perceive or think. God sits outside of our human senses. So the mind set on Christ is not limited to what can be measured by the senses.

That doesn't mean God ignores or bypasses your human senses. It means what you see, hear, and feel are not all there is. What you think is not all there is.

There's a very good reason the person with a kingdom mind is not bound by human limitations. It's called revelation. First Corinthians 2:10 says we know the things of God because He has revealed them to us. Revelation gives us the glasses we need to see what is otherwise too far away for us.

Without the divine visual assistance called revelation, the kingdom would be very blurry for us. It wouldn't come into clear focus. Without the mind of Christ, we would live our lives only by what we see up close.

We need assistance to help us see life as it really is, so we can think kingdom thoughts and live kingdom lives.

## A DIVINE VIEWPOINT

A kingdom mind is not only outside of human limitations. It also functions the very opposite of the way a natural, or unsaved, mind functions. Paul continued in 1 Corinthians 2:

> But a natural man does not accept the things of the
> Spirit of God, for they are foolishness to him; and he
> cannot understand them, because they are spiritually
> appraised. But he who is spiritual appraises all things,
> yet he himself is appraised by no one. (vv. 14–15)

When I talk about a kingdom mind, I am talking about
a mind that looks at all of reality from a spiritual or divine
viewpoint. A person with a kingdom mind views life through
the glasses of the Holy Spirit.

You have probably seen people who wear sunglasses as
a fashion accent—for style only. They even have a way of
putting on their shades that tells you they are merely styling
when they wear them.

I'm afraid some believers come to church for style. They're
looking the part, but their divine glasses are just a fashion accent. They're not operating with a kingdom mind, so they're
not pursuing a kingdom agenda.

Carrying your Bible under your arm doesn't guarantee
you a kingdom mind. Neither does going through religious
rituals. You know you have a kingdom mind when you sift all
of your decisions through a divine mindset.

When you have a kingdom mind and you face a decision,
you raise certain questions. What does Christ think about

this? How would He react to this? What does Christ want me to do here? Operating with a spiritual mentality links you up to God's "Internet" so you can tap into His thinking on your decision.

This is diametrically opposed to the way the unsaved think. Paul tells us the natural person thinks spiritual things are foolishness. The unsaved person ridicules the things of the Spirit because he cannot understand them. He doesn't have the antenna to receive them.

But since the natural mind is not our focus here, let's talk about believers. Even we who have the antenna to receive the things of the Spirit can have technical problems. And if we don't fix the problem, we can waste a lot of time and cause ourselves a lot of frustration fiddling with the wrong thing.

We were having problems with our television reception some years ago. I fooled with the buttons on the set, trying to get a good picture. I looked at the directions that came with the TV. But no matter what I did, I couldn't get clear reception.

The reason is I was starting in the wrong place. My problem was not with the TV, but on my roof. The repairman I had to call told me my antenna had been knocked around by a recent storm. It needed to be turned back toward the signal.

Now that helped a lot, but it didn't completely fix the trouble because, as the man told me, I had a second problem. Our house is in a gully amid lots of tall trees.

The trees were interfering with the signal, so the repairman had to put an extension on our antenna to lift it above the interference so it could receive the signal clearly. Once he turned and raised the antenna, the picture was fine.

Maybe you can see where I'm heading with this. It's easy to fiddle with the buttons in our lives, trying to get a clear picture of this thing called life.

But that's starting in the wrong place. Until the antenna of your mind is turned toward the divine signal, messing with the other stuff in your life won't help. That signal is coming from a King who has a kingdom agenda for you, and when you get that signal straight, life's picture will clear up.

You say, "But, Tony, I'm really trying to develop a kingdom mind. I really believe I have my antenna turned in the right direction, but the signal doesn't seem to be coming through."

Maybe you've got too many trees around you blocking the reception. Daily stuff like a job, finances, family problems, houses that need paint, and cars that need tires can grow up and crowd out God's signal. The answer is not to cut down the trees but to raise your antenna above them.

If you will get your mind tuned to the divine signal and lifted up above the "trees" of circumstances and other people, you will get the right picture, the divine viewpoint.

Now you can see why the unsaved person can't do either one of these things. He doesn't even have an antenna. But the problem is not just ignorance. According to Romans 1:18–23, unsaved people have corrupted their minds on purpose.

They know the truth but they suppress it so they can sin. Genesis 6:5 says before the flood, every thought of men's minds was totally wicked. So God gave the unsaved over to a "depraved mind" (Romans 1:28).

## THE MIND OF CHRIST

What a contrast we see back in 1 Corinthians 2:16: "But we have the mind of Christ."

At conversion you got a new mind. A new program was inserted into your soul through the life-giving work of the Holy Spirit.

But some of us have been so used to running the old program that we have problems getting the new program installed and running. The solution is to make sure your spirit is plugged into God's Spirit.

Remember we're not talking about salvation. We're talking about living like the kingdom people we are. Here's what I mean.

In 1 Corinthians 2:11, Paul asked, "Who among men knows the thoughts of a man except the spirit of the man, which is in him? Even so the thoughts of God no one knows except the Spirit of God." Then he said in verse 12, "Now we have received, not the spirit of the world, but the Spirit who is from God."

The idea is this: Since no one knows God's thoughts like

God's Spirit, and no one knows your thoughts like your spirit, the key is to link your spirit with God's Spirit.

To put it another way, if you want your thoughts to be saturated with God's thoughts, your spirit has to be in tune with His Spirit so His thoughts are transferred to your thoughts.

## THE BATTLE FOR YOUR MIND

The Communist government of China has special labor camps for political and religious prisoners whose thinking and ideas are considered a threat to the Marxist cause. A number of Chinese pastors and other Christian leaders have been sentenced to these camps, sometimes for years at a time.

The Chinese have an interesting term for this process. They say the prisoner is being sent to the camp for "reeducation through labor," a pitiful euphemism for an attempt to break prisoners down physically and reprogram their minds through propaganda. The idea is to do whatever it takes to try to remake the prisoner in the Communists' image.

The Chinese government's "reeducation" camps operate on a basic principle that is taught in God's Word, except the Communists are using it for their twisted, evil purposes. The principle is this: If you want people to think in new ways and in different categories, you have to erase the old ways of thinking from their minds. Their minds must be reprogrammed.

The Chinese Communists are deadly serious about their propaganda program because they know the survival of Marxism depends on capturing people's minds. Even one pastor with a renewed mind, or a political leader who is committed to democracy, is a potential threat to their system.

Like the Chinese, we have an enemy who seeks to influence, and even control, our minds. The more influence Satan has over your mind, the easier it is for him to take you down the wrong path and get you sidetracked from fulfilling God's agenda for your life.

Since our minds are so crucial to our functioning as Christians, we must understand the relationship of our souls with our minds because our soul is what makes us who we are. Your soul is *you*. It comprises not only your mind but also your emotions and your will. These three gather together to make up your soul.

You are not your body. Your body is simply a container for your soul. Your soul is your essence. When a person dies, that soul is what will either go to heaven or to hell. The key to experiencing a kingdom life takes place within our soul because our soul is what has been created for eternity.

## SIN'S EFFECT ON OUR SOULS

The problem with our souls is they have been contaminated since birth, making them distorted. Have you ever been to an amusement park and seen the mirrors that make you look fat, super-skinny, tall, short, or crooked? This is what has happened to our souls. To varying degrees, the penetration and effects of sin have engrafted themselves into our souls. The soul needs to be fixed, but the difficulty is the soul can't fix itself.

Most of the time we are trying to get the soul to fix the soul, but that works just as well as getting distortion to fix distortion. I call this approach soul management. Soul management is when we spend time, energy, and money trying to make our souls better. We make resolutions and promises tied to the soul and its influence on our body. We listen to sermons, cross off our lists, and come up with plans on what we can do to manage our soul.

But God doesn't want us to focus on managing the distortion. Distortion will always be distortion, no matter how well it is managed. What God offers is soul transformation. Sure, we might be able to manage certain parts of our soul for certain lengths of time to certain degrees, but our soul can never deliver itself, make itself better, or set itself free. Only Jesus can do that. Jesus died on the cross not just to take your soul to heaven, but also to deliver your soul in history.

But before deliverance can occur, a death must occur. Jesus said that if we want to be His disciples, we must "take up" our "cross daily" and follow Him (Luke 9:23). The cross symbolizes an instrument of death.

In order for your soul to become fully alive, it must first die. And it will need to die daily. Every morning when you wake up, don't think about how you can manage your soul. Instead, think about what part of your soul is not in alignment with God and ask Him to let that part die. As long as you try to keep your soul alive, it will continue to be distorted. You will never experience the freedom in life that you were meant to experience by your Creator until your soul dies.

The soul within you that needs to die is your self-life, your viewpoint on a matter, the very thoughts that make up your mind.

## THE NEW LIFE INSIDE

Not only does your soul need to die, a new life needs to grow. This new life first comes to you as a seed. When you trusted Jesus Christ as your Savior for the forgiveness of your sins, you received what the Bible calls, a "seed" that is "imperishable" (1 Peter 1:23). This is your new nature.

But there are many Christians who have this seed and are still wondering why the Christian life doesn't seem to be working. They try their hand at soul management but end up being frustrated because the results are only temporary. The reason why the seed is not working to bring about transformation is because the seed has not been allowed to expand.

The expansion of the seed affects the control of the soul.

The self-life will continue to rule, even though you have the spirit-life within you, because the spirit-life is still in seed form. Any time you have a seed and that seed is not planted, it will not express life. It has life, but it won't express life. A two-week-old fetus in a mother's womb has all of the DNA within it for its fullest potential of life. But that two-week-old fetus doesn't express life like a full-grown baby just after delivery. Because the baby is now the result of the seed expanded.

## QUICK TO HEAR, SLOW TO SPEAK

James writes, "This you know, my beloved brethren. But everyone must be quick to hear, slow to speak and slow to anger . . ." (James 1:19). The first thing I want to point out before we move further into this passage is that James is talking to Christians. He calls them "beloved brethren." So these verses only apply to those who have trusted Christ for their salvation.

James follows his introduction with a command. He says everyone—so that includes all of us—must be quick to hear, slow to speak, and slow to anger.

The question you might be asking is this: Quick to hear what? We will find out a few verses later in the passage that we are to be quick to hear God's point of view on a matter. The other question you might be asking is this: Slow to speak what? We are to be slow to speak our point of view on a matter. And when God's point of view on a matter differs from our point of view, we are told to be slow to anger about it.

However, we often flip it and do the opposite. We are quick to espouse our viewpoint on a matter and slow to hear His point of view. Which is why we go to everyone else first to find out what they think we should do before we go to God. But God says we should be quick to receive His point of view.

## RECEIVE THE WORD IMPLANTED

We read this as James continues. He says, "Therefore, putting aside all filthiness and all that remains of wickedness, in humility receive the word implanted, which is able to save your souls" (James 1:21).

But wait a minute. These people are already saved. He just called them his "beloved brethren." Yet he is still saying that their souls need to be "saved." This is because when you and I trusted Christ for the forgiveness of our sins, our souls were saved *eternally*. But our souls were not saved, transformed, automatically in *history*.

When you got saved, you brought your issues to the cross. You brought your past, your bondage, addictions, propensities, and problems to the cross. Jesus saved you for heaven in a flicker of time. But He saves you on earth progressively. First Corinthians 1:18 says that, "the word of the cross is foolishness . . . but to us who are being saved" it is power. In that verse we clearly see His reference to us as "being saved"—being transformed.

He says, "receive the word implanted, which is able to save your souls" (James 1:21). First, remove anything that will interfere with the expansion of the word implanted. Because the new nature, which is consistent with the word of God, has been implanted in your soul in seed form. God says to receive it because receiving it is the key to the saving of your soul—your self-life—the real you, on earth.

One of the reasons why we are not being delivered or experiencing victory even though we want to do better, desire to do better, and promise to do better as children of the King is because the implanted seed has not been received. God says if you will ever receive what has been implanted within you, it will deliver your soul.

## LIKE AN EGG IN A MOTHER'S WOMB

The implanted word can be best illustrated by comparing it to a fertilized egg in the womb of a woman. The fertilized egg has been planted there in the uterus. It is set there to receive the nourishment coming to it from an outside source.

The woman eats and the nourishment from her food goes down the umbilical cord. The nutrients necessary for growth and development reach into the womb of the woman and enable the fertilized egg within her to grow.

Just like the fertilized egg requires nourishment to grow becoming a fully developed baby ready for delivery, the seed that has been implanted in us also requires nourishment. The written word of God must reach into the depth of our soul where the implanted word abides with the imperishable seed in order for that seed to expand and the life of Christ to be expressed. The only tool designed to expand the seed located in the soul is the word of God. There are no other tools.

But you say, wait a minute, Tony. I've been coming to church for years. I've been reading my Bible for years. My soul has not changed. Or it changes for a while and then goes back to how it was before. Why isn't it working for me?

The answer to your question is found in the word "receive." It is possible to have the word implanted but to still not receive it. The word "receive" means to welcome. It means more than simply hearing something, having something, or knowing something. It means to welcome it.

When you welcome someone who is standing at the door of your home, you invite that person in. That person is now within your home. You didn't stand at the door and say, "you are welcome." You ushered that person in, which enabled your welcome to be experienced and lived out.

When we welcome the word of God, it goes to work in our souls. In chapter 4, verse 12, of the book of Hebrews it says, "For the word of God is living and active and sharper than any two-edged sword, and piercing as far as the division of soul and spirit, of both joints and marrow, and able to judge the thoughts and intentions of the heart."

Let's talk a minute about the "word." We just read that the word of God is alive. The Greek word used there is "logos." It means the living word. It is the word referred to in John 1:1 that says, "In the beginning was the Word, and the Word was with God, and the Word was God." It is the energized life-giving word of God.

The Bible calls this word food for the soul. Just like you have food for the body that supplies proper nutrition to enable your body to function well, there is also food for the soul. The Bible is to the soul what food is to the body. Jesus said that man should not "live on bread alone, but on every word that proceeds out of the mouth of God" (Matthew 4:4).

The book of Hebrews tells us when this food reaches where it needs to in our soul, it pierces as far as the division of our soul and spirit. But in order for it to do that, it needs to be received.

To be received means it has to reach further than your ears. Hearing a sermon on Sunday is good, but if it doesn't go further than your ears it won't do the work of transforming your soul.

Do you remember reading in the Bible when Jesus would say, "He who has ears to hear, let him hear" (Matthew 11:15)? He's not talking about simply being able to hear it spoken. Or about reading it in a book. Or reading it in your Bible. Jesus is saying to hear it in such a manner that you receive it. Receive the word so it can penetrate to the level of the division of soul and spirit.

What is the soul? Remember I said earlier it is the *you*, your essence. It is your mind, emotions, and will. What is the spirit? That is God. That is the seed He has implanted in you. Your new nature. When the word gets down to the level it needs to, it is going to make a distinction between what is you and what is God.

It will divide what is your life and what is God's life. What are your thoughts and what are God's thoughts. What are your feelings and what are God's feelings. What is your choice and what is God's choice. It is going to make a distinction between the two.

The writer of Hebrews goes on to say it will judge the thoughts and intentions of the heart. The heart is the center of the soul that pumps direction to every part of our life. The word is only received when it has reached into the depth of your heart—your life center.

Which means if you read this book today and it works its way to your head and you say, "Tony, I understand what you're talking about," or it works its way to your emotions and you say, "Yes, I feel what you are writing about," or it works its way to your will and you say, "I know a decision that I need to make," but it doesn't get to the heart, it hasn't arrived at its destination. And if it hasn't arrived at its destination, it hasn't been received.

As the seed expands in your soul, it will begin to dominate your thoughts, feelings, and will so actions which reflect the viewpoint of God will become natural to you in your daily life. That's the difference. They won't be reactions you have based on a sermon, chapter, or devotional you read that morning.

The writer of Hebrews illustrates the word of God as a two-edged sword. It has two parts. It is both destructive and constructive. Anyone who has ever remodeled or added on to a house can understand this. In order to build something up when you remodel a house, you must first tear something down. The word of God also seeks to tear stuff down in order to make room for the expansion of the seed.

## THE NATURE OF THE BATTLE

Paul wrote, "The weapons of our warfare are not of the flesh, but divinely powerful for the destruction of fortresses" (2 Corinthians 10:4). This word *fortresses* is key to understanding and winning the battle for your mind. You will never be successful in allowing the seed to expand and the Holy Spirit to reprogram your mind until the enemy's fortresses in your mind are torn down.

## SATAN'S STRONGHOLDS

What are these fortresses Paul was talking about? The King James Version calls them "strongholds." You've probably seen a fortress in a movie about medieval times. Picture a huge structure made of stone with high walls and towers surrounded by a moat.

Medieval fortresses were built to be impregnable. Just looking up at those massive walls would be intimidating to an enemy soldier standing outside, let alone thinking of trying to scale the walls with ladders and bring the fortress down. Now transfer that image to the realm of the mind, and you'll have the idea.

God says these strongholds have to be destroyed, so that means He didn't build them. A stronghold is a negative, destructive pattern of thinking developed in our minds either through repetition, or traumatic experiences, or other circumstances. As the old adage says, when you sow a thought, you reap an act; sow an act and you reap a habit; sow a habit, and you reap a character; sow a character, and you reap a destiny.

Once the stronghold is built, it gives the enemy a place to launch further attacks against your mind and a fortification to repel your attempts to dislodge him. One reason strongholds are so powerful is they are so entrenched.

Satan builds a stronghold when he convinces a person his

situation is hopeless, he is a drug addict, negative person, controlled by fear, or an alcoholic by nature, and will never be anything else. Once a person starts believing that, it's pretty much all over because we will always act in accord with who we believe we are.

You can tell when people are being oppressed by a stronghold. They say things like, "I can't help myself," "It's not my fault," "I was born this way," or "I'm just a victim."

When we view something as unchangeable that God says is changeable, the enemy has built a stronghold in our minds. It doesn't have to be anything as dramatic as drug addiction or alcoholism. Many of us have strongholds of hopelessness, jealousy, lust, or anger.

What needs to be done with these strongholds?

The only solution is to tear those lofty strongholds down by "taking every thought captive to the obedience to Christ" (2 Corinthians 10:5). This is how to reprogram your mind.

Why must we take every thought captive to Christ? Because our souls are distorted, and we need to align our thoughts with God's thoughts. We have to capture and test our thoughts with God's viewpoint on the matter because if we don't receive His word and welcome it into our hearts, we will continue to live defeated lives based on outward efforts at transformation.

In fact, we are told in the book of Romans it is in the act of our mind becoming renewed we attain the victory God has called us to in life. We read, "Do not conform to the pattern of this world, but be transformed by the renewing of your mind. Then you will be able to test and approve what God's will is—his good, pleasing and perfect will" (Romans 12:2, NIV).

Remember, our soul is distorted. Our soul cannot fix our soul. We need to put to death our viewpoint on whatever matter we are facing in our lives that is holding us captive. Then we need to receive God's life-giving viewpoint on the matter and renew our minds according to His truth. If and when we do not allow a complete renewing of our minds with God's truth, we wind up with double-mindedness which produces a form of spiritual schizophrenia that keeps us from maximizing or benefiting from the kingdom of God.

In order to avoid this double-mindedness, you must set your mind on Christ. Colossians 3:1–2 says:

> Therefore, if you have been raised up with Christ, keep seeking the things above, where Christ is, seated at the right hand of God. Set your mind on the things above, not on the things that are on earth.

Where you set your mind is so important because what you set your mind on will penetrate and dominate your thinking. One day the way I viewed my circumstances completely changed due to a renewed mind. I was in the sixth grade at Alexander Hamilton Elementary School in Baltimore. We had a bully at our school—a huge guy who was basically eighteen in the sixth grade. You know the type.

This bully decided he didn't like me, and one day he threatened to get me after school. I was terrified. When the final bell rang I took off out of the school, but he spotted me and took off after me.

I knew a truth he didn't know: I lived just three blocks from the school. That truth definitely ignited me to have the faith that I could outrun the bully and make it home before he pounded me into the pavement.

I've never been all that fast, but on that day I would have qualified for the Olympics. The bully was closing in on me, but I turned into my front yard and shot into the house before he could catch me. I ran all the way upstairs to my room and collapsed.

I was still feeling fearful. My heart was pounding from fear and my three-block Olympic sprint. But soon my heart slowed down because of a new fact. I was in my house. The bully couldn't get me there. My faith kicked in, so to speak, and I started feeling safe.

Then another truth dawned on me. Not only was I safe at home in my room, but my dad was home too. That was great, because even if the bully came to my door, he would have to deal with my dad. So now my faith was really getting ignited.

Before long I was so full of faith I started walking all over the house as if I was really in charge. I could walk around with inner security and confidence because the truth of my situation had changed my thinking and my mind, which changed my feelings and affected my feet.

If you belong to Christ, you may feel like the enemy is always out there trying to chase you down. But when you set your mind on the things of Christ, you can receive God's word and allow it to act as a two-edged sword in your life. Ask the Holy Spirit to reprogram your mind with the truth of His Word, and then start acting in light of that. Not only will your fears and doubts leave when you come to trust and stand on God's promises in His Word, but God will build strongholds of truth in your mind and man the guard towers Himself.

That's exactly what He promised in His Word. "The peace of God, which surpasses all comprehension, will guard your hearts and your minds in Christ Jesus" (Philippians 4:7). That word "guard" means "to do sentry duty, to stand guard." In Colossians 3:15, Paul said God's peace will "rule" in our hearts. Could you use a little peace in your life right now?

Don't ever buy Satan's lie that your situation is hopeless or unchangeable. The truth is, "[You] can do all things through Him who strengthens [you]" (Philippians 4:13).

But this begins by focusing on your identity in Christ and your relationship with Him. You need to live the way Paul described in Colossians 3:3: "You have died and your life is hidden with Christ in God." He added in verse 4 that Christ is our life.

If your mind is not set on Christ, you are not treating Him as though He is your life. God called David a man after His own heart (Acts 13:22) because David couldn't get God off his mind. In the Psalms David said God was the first thing on his mind when he woke up. He couldn't get God off his mind all day. And during the night watches, when everybody else was asleep, David would wake up with thoughts of God on his mind (Psalm 63:6).

Such passion makes a difference in the way you live. When Jesus Christ dominates your mind, your hands don't have to do what they used to do. Your feet don't have to go where they used to go. Your mouth doesn't have to say what it used to say.

Your mind doesn't have room for Christ *and* the world. You are either going to think about Christ *or* about the world. A kingdom mind is a mind firmly fixed on Jesus Christ and the unchanging Word of God.

# THE URBAN ALTERNATIVE

D r. Tony Evans and The Urban Alternative (TUA) equips, empowers, and unites Christians to impact individuals, families, churches, and communities to restore hope and transform lives.

We believe the core cause of the problems we face in our personal lives, homes, churches, and societies is a spiritual one; therefore, the only way to address them is spiritually. We've tried a political, a social, an economic, and even a religious agenda. It's time for a Kingdom Agenda—God's visible and comprehensive rule over every area of life—because when we function as we were designed, there is a divine power that changes everything. It renews and restores as the life of Christ is made manifest within our own. As we align ourselves under Him, there is an alignment that happens from deep within—where He brings about full restoration. It is an atmosphere that revives and makes whole.

As it impacts us, it impacts others—transforming every sphere of life in which we live. When each biblical sphere of life functions in accordance with God's Word, the outcomes are evangelism, discipleship, and community impact. As we learn how to govern ourselves under God, we then transform the institutions of family, church, and society from a biblically based kingdom perspective. Where through Him, we are touching heaven and changing earth.

To achieve our goal we use a variety of strategies, methods, and resources for reaching and equipping as many people as possible.

## BROADCAST MEDIA

Hundreds of thousands of individuals experience *The Alternative with Dr. Tony Evans* through the daily radio broadcast playing on nearly 1,000 radio outlets and in over 130 countries. The broadcast can also be seen on several television networks and is viewable online at TonyEvans.org.

## LEADERSHIP TRAINING

*The Kingdom Agenda Pastors (KAP)* provides a *viable network* for *like-minded pastors* who embrace the Kingdom Agenda philosophy. Pastors have the opportunity to go deeper with Dr. Tony Evans as they are given greater biblical knowledge, practical applications, and resources to impact individuals, families, churches, and communities. KAP welcomes *senior and associate pastors* of all churches.

*The Kingdom Agenda Pastors' Summit* progressively develops church leaders to meet the demands of the 21st century while maintaining the Gospel message and the strategic position of the church. The Summit introduces *intensive seminars, workshops,* and *resources*, addressing issues affecting the community, family, leadership, organizational health, and more.

*Pastors' Wives Ministry*, founded by Dr. Lois Evans, provides *counsel, encouragement,* and *spiritual resources* for pastors' wives as they serve with their husbands in the ministry. A primary focus of the ministry is the KAP Summit that offers senior pastors' wives a safe place to *reflect, renew,* and *relax* along with training in personal development, spiritual growth, and care for their emotional and physical well-being.

## COMMUNITY IMPACT

*National Church Adopt-A-School Initiative (NCAASI)* prepares churches across the country to impact communities by using *public schools as the primary vehicle for effecting positive social change* in urban youth and families. Leaders of churches, school districts, faith-based organizations, and other nonprofit organizations are equipped with the knowledge and tools to *forge partnerships* and build *strong social service delivery systems*. This training is based on the comprehensive church-based community impact strategy conducted by Oak Cliff Bible Fellowship. It addresses such areas as economic development, education, housing, health revitalization, family renewal, and racial reconciliation. We also assist churches in tailoring the model to meet the specific needs of their communities while simultaneously addressing the spiritual and moral frame of reference.

## RESOURCE DEVELOPMENT

We are fostering lifelong learning partnerships with the people we serve by providing a variety of published materials. We offer booklets, Bible studies, books, CDs, and DVDs to strengthen people in their walk with God and ministry to others.

\* \* \*

For more information, a catalog of Dr. Tony Evans'
ministry resources, and a complimentary copy of
Dr. Evans' devotional newsletter,
call (800) 800-3222,
or write TUA at P.O. Box 4000, Dallas TX 75208,
or log on to
TonyEvans.org.

# The Life Under God Series

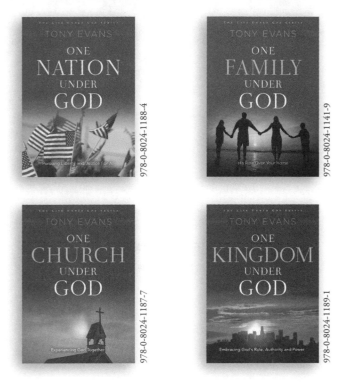

**God's Word offers a biblically based kingdom agenda.**
In The Life Under God series, Dr. Tony Evans highlights the four
areas which God has entrusted to us—personal, family, church,
and society—and demonstrates that Scripture has provided a clear
authority and a comprehensive approach to all of life.

MORE INFORMATION AVAILABLE AT THEKINGDOMAGENDABOOK.COM

# Tony EVANS
## THE URBAN ALTERNATIVE

At The Urban Alternative, the national ministry of Dr. Tony Evans, we seek to restore hope and transform lives to reflect the values of the kingdom of God. Along with our community outreach initiative, leadership training and family and personal growth emphasis, Dr. Evans continues to minister to people from the pulpit to the heart as the relevant expositor with the powerful voice. Lives are touched both locally and abroad through our daily radio broadcast, weekly television ministry and internet access points.

# Presenting an
# ALTERNATIVE to:

## Community Outreach

Equipping leaders to engage public schools and communities with mentoring, family support services and a commitment to a brighter tomorrow.

## Leadership Training

Offering an exclusive opportunity for pastors and their wives to receive discipleship from Drs. Tony and Lois Evans and the TUA staff, along with networking opportunities, resources and encouragement.

## Family and Personal Growth

Strengthening homes and deepening spiritual lives through helpful resources that encourage hope and health for the glory of God.

TonyEvans.org

# urbanpraise

**Urban Praise**, a commercial-free Moody Radio Internet station, offers a soulful blend of rich gospel and urban music. Energize your faith with artists like Kirk Franklin, Israel Houghton, Shirley Caesar, CeCe Winans, Walter Hawkins, and Lecrae, along with bite-size teaching segments from Tony Evans, Crawford Loritts, Melvin Banks, Beth Moore, and others.

**www.urbanpraiseradio.org**

MOODYRADIO
*Where you turn. For life.*

# MOODYRADIO

*Where you turn. For life.*

Moody Radio produces and delivers compelling programs filled with biblical insights and creative expressions of faith that help you take the next step in your relationship with Christ.

You can hear Moody Radio on 36 stations and more than 1,500 radio outlets across the U.S. and Canada. Or listen on your smartphone with the Moody Radio app!

**www.moodyradio.org**